*Dedicated to all
who serve.*

God bless and keep you.

Contents

7. Family Ties

8. Life Changes

Acknowledgments

As a big fan of the Academy Awards, I have practiced my Oscar acceptance speech for decades—and every year it gets shorter and shorter. Not because there are less people to thank—but because the older I get the more certain I become that God is in control of everything. Ultimately He is the one who must be acknowledged for every good and perfect gift—and if I ever do win that Oscar, you can bet I'll be praising His name from the podium—whether it's accepted protocol or not.

That's why my acknowledgment list will be short in this, the seventeenth book under the God Allows U-Turns brand umbrella. Every step of the way God has opened doors to make this very special book happen. He laid the idea on my heart years ago. From the first volume in the God Allows U-Turns series, I've wanted to share military stories like those you'll find within the pages of this collection. God orchestrated story submissions from every branch of the military in record time, and He has a plan for sharing this book with readers around the world. If ever there was a "God Project," this is it. Thank You, Lord, for answering my prayer to bring this book to fruition. Thank you, Harvest House Publishers, for grasping the vision. Thank you, readers, for sharing this book with your family and friends.

I'd like to acknowledge the Protestant Women of the Chapel (PWOC) during this their fiftieth year in praying for the brave men and women serving our great nation. May the prayers of this formidable group of women continue to be answered as you stand firm on God's promise to hear when you call.

There's simply no way I can list everyone who played a part in making this book possible—thank you from the bottom of my heart to everyone who had a part. A special thank you must go to Cheryll Hutchings, Jennifer Devlin, Nick Harrison, Terri McPherson, Ramona Richards, Sharen Watson, Jennifer Carey, Steve Laube, and my dear husband, Kevin Bottke. What gifts from God each of you are.

And a heartfelt thank you to the courageous men and women of our military, and to their families and friends, for sharing these powerful and poignant stories with us. You are gifts to us all. God bless you, and God bless America.

Allison Bottke

*Therefore I tell you, whatever you ask for in prayer,
believe that you have received it, and it will be yours.*

Mark 11:24

Introduction

From the moment they put on their respective uniforms, they are no longer our children, spouses, neighbors, or friends. They become our country's front line of defense with one sole function—to protect our great nation—at any cost. These brave men and women strive to fulfill their duties with whatever it takes, even to the extent of sacrificing their lives. While they may use the latest weapons and receive the best of training, for many, the most important piece of armor is the powerful act of prayer.

When we began compiling this special anthology, our greatest fear was to find we might not have enough stories to fill an entire volume. After reading stacks and stacks of submitted stories, our fear quickly turned to astonishment—it seemed the "answered prayer" theme struck a chord. It became clear that military men and women around the globe, as well as their families and friends, were gaining great strength in these challenging times as God answered the prayers of their hearts. How were we ever going to narrow them down to fill just one book?

The real-life short stories in *God Answers Prayers—Military Edition* provide a powerful and passionate look at how prayer can protect, inspire, encourage, change, and heal. God has been answering prayers in the military environment for countless years, throughout numerous challenges in our country's history. We are humbled to share many of these timeless stories with you now, as we come face-to-face with people who put their trust in God, experiencing His presence to calm the storm or to answer some of life's most difficult questions. Along with sharing their own heartfelt prayers during times of war and peace, you will find stories of intercessory prayers from spouses, family, friends, and their brothers- and sisters-in-arms.

Within the pages of this book, you will find just how awesome the power of prayer can truly be. Not all the true stories are about combat and fighting; some feature everyday matters we all could face, but with the added responsibility of having to put your country first and your loved ones second—making simple decisions infinitely more complex.

No matter which branch of the military served, or what race, gender, or creed, the contributing authors who share from their hearts all know God is their first line of defense.

Due to the current struggle overseas with many servicemen and servicewomen being deployed, we want to share with readers around the world how God is helping and comforting these brave souls and their families—in all branches of the military—how He has done so in the past and continues to do so today.

We dedicate this book to the men and women who have served and continue to serve our great nation. May God bless them and answer the prayers of their hearts.

Allison Bottke
Cheryll Hutchings
Jennifer Devlin

1

In the Presence of My Enemies

Aᴄᴄᴏʀᴅɪɴɢ ᴛᴏ ᴀɴ ᴏʟᴅ sᴀʏɪɴɢ, "There are no atheists in foxholes." It's funny what God will do to get our attention, even to the point of linking us up with praying people in the middle of dangerous situations. Those are true "Come to Jesus" moments, when you can see His hand of protection and mercy at work. To think about a soldier praying for something other than to come out alive may seem strange to people who don't believe, but those very prayers have ushered new believers before the throne of God. Prayers for wisdom, guidance, and discernment in the midst of danger often show the depth of God's love flowing through those physically standing in the gap, risking everything for our freedom.

❧❧❧

But you are a shield around me, O Lᴏʀᴅ;
you bestow glory on me and lift up my head.

Psᴀʟᴍ 3:3

∽ *Faith and Hope in a Land of Heartbreak* ∾

Audrey Kletscher Helbling, Faribault, Minnesota

The year was 1953.

High on a rock pile in the mountains of Korea, a sniper perched, methodically picking off American soldiers one by one. Day after day more men fell. Blood stained the soil of Heartbreak Ridge, a rugged seven-mile stretch of unforgiving, mountainous terrain that had become a killing field.

Below the ridge, a young foot soldier hunkered down on the ground, ever watchful for the shooter who had killed so many of his comrades. He had been just nine days shy of his twenty-second birthday when his sergeant handed him a sniper rifle. "Kletscher, it's your turn today," the officer said to the young soldier. That soldier—my dad—grasped the weapon and prepared to follow orders.

For days now he had stayed in the trenches, watching, studying the sniper's shooting pattern. With gun in hand, my dad had a shot at taking out the enemy. As he peeked over the edge of the trench, a bullet whizzed toward him and landed with a thud in the earthen wall. The angle of the slug gave away the sniper's position. Raising his arms, my dad carefully aligned his rifle, and then fired. Ka-puck! The bullet hit its intended target.

Two days later, a dozen men were ordered to retrieve the dead sniper. They approached cautiously, concerned that the frozen body could be booby trapped. My dad stood guard nearby, watching for enemies who might sneak in behind them. The soldiers made it back to their posts without incident.

Suddenly they came under heavy attack as mortar rounds lobbed toward them. As my dad lifted his head to see where the shells were landing, he was hit in the face and neck by shrapnel. "I knew blood was running," he said. "But there was nothing I could do. You don't run." Scared, shaking, and badly bleeding, he settled in for a long night. Just then two more mortars sailed in, landing next to him. They failed to explode. If they had blown on impact, my father would have died, another casualty of war.

"It was that guardian angel again," he said, pointing heavenward. He offered no further explanation.

For months my dad had been shadowed by his guardian angel as he patrolled the no-man's land of Korea. In a land of bone-chilling bitter cold, this young farmer from Minnesota dug his boots deep into foxholes, sought refuge behind bunkers and in trenches, witnessed aerial dogfights, dodged gunfire and bombs, endured days of nonstop shelling, and engaged in fierce combat along the front line. Always he prayed his life would be spared and he would return safely home.

Home was always on the minds of the soldiers, including my dad. In a letter written to his parents on March 4, 1953, his twenty-second birthday, my dad mentioned nothing about the shrapnel injuries he had suffered a week earlier. In fact, he told his parents, "I'm feeling fine, don't worry about me." He expressed concern for his younger brother, who might be drafted. He worried how his parents would manage the family farm with one less pair of hands. He also wrote about his faith: "Sure was good to go to church. I had communion. I always try and make every church service they got over here. Once a week the chaplain comes up here on the hill. It's always good to go. Always makes a guy know he isn't alone." Photos my dad snapped of church services in Korea show soldiers kneeling in the dirt, receiving the Lord's Supper before an outdoor makeshift altar.

Even when he was alone, my dad felt God's presence. He carried with him a small black book, *God Our Refuge,* a gift from the women's group in his home church. It included gospel readings, devotions, meditations, prayers, hymns, and more. The edges of the

American soldiers receive the Lord's Supper at chapel services near the front line in Korea, May 1953.   (Photo by Elvern A. Kletscher)

book are grimy and curled inward, softened from months in my dad's pocket. Inside the slim volume my dad found solace, hope, and comfort in the face of constant death.

With men dying all around him, dad moved up quickly in military rank, replacing those who had fallen. Ever vigilant, he never lost a man under his direct command. "I wanted to come home, and I wanted them to come home," he said.

But not everyone made it back to U.S. soil. The death of one soldier, in particular, haunted my father throughout his life. My dad had just returned from the front line when his regiment was ordered to dig trenches in a second line of defense.

Before leaving for the assignment, my dad learned a fellow sergeant would be shipping out the next day, headed back to Nebraska. Everyone was excited for the young man, especially since he would be returning home to a six-week-old daughter he had never seen.

Those happy thoughts were on the soldiers' minds as they moved forward. Then it happened. "Just as we got in the trenches, I heard a round coming in," my dad said. "I knew someone would get hit." Before his eyes, my father saw his young friend blown to pieces by an incoming shell.

"I could fight a lot, but that one hurt," he said, fighting back tears.

It was a horrific battlefield memory my dad carried with him for the rest of his life. It's a memory that gave him nightmares until his death fifty years later. It's one of the few memories he ever shared of a war that claimed 33,650 American lives.

Twenty-eight men from the 2nd Battalion, 65th Infantry Regiment, my dad's unit, died during the early summer of 1953. On July 31, my dad attended a service in Sucham-dong, Korea, memorializing the twenty-eight soldiers, among them his buddy from Nebraska. My dad found comfort in these words from John 15:13 printed in the service folder: "Greater love has no man than this, that a man lay down his life for his friends" (RSV). He carried that memorial bulletin with him all the way home from Korea. It was a remembrance of those who had fought beside him and given the ultimate sacrifice—their lives.

While the Korean War is often termed "The Forgotten War," sandwiched between World War II and the Vietnam War, it was never a forgotten war for my father. During his time on Korean soil, my dad saw more blood and death than anyone should witness in a lifetime. He carried the bodies of his buddies off the battlefields in a land that chilled his bones to the very marrow. More than two-thirds of the Americans who died—23,835 of them—were killed, like my dad's friend, on the battlefield.

Almost a year after his feet touched Korean soil at the port of Inchon, my dad boarded a ship for America. He was returning home a different man, a man whose emotions and body had been scarred by the horrors of war. He had seen too much blood, too much death, and too many atrocities. He had lived in a land so cold water froze in canteens, oil congealed in soldiers' weapons, and the frozen bodies of comrades were used to barricade positions.

Despite everything, my dad's single most earnest prayer had been answered. God had brought him safely back from the mountainous killing fields of Korea to the flat, open farm fields of southwestern Minnesota. For that he was thankful.

Forty-seven years later the United States government thanked my dad for serving his country in a war that many forgot. On May 21, 2000, he received a Purple Heart for the wounds he suffered at Heartbreak Ridge on February 26, 1953. For reasons unknown, my dad never got his medal as a young soldier.

That Sunday afternoon in May 2000 was a memorable day for my dad and his family. Emotions overflowed as the Purple Heart was pinned on his chest. I choked back tears as I focused my camera, intent on capturing this intensely personal, yet public, moment. Tears slipped down my dad's face as he recounted war stories to a local television reporter covering the event. The pain in his eyes was obvious as he spoke. He was proud of his service to his country, yet the horrific battlefield memories were still almost too unbearable to share.

But it was his faith that sustained him through the years—first as a young soldier fighting in the mountains of Korea, and in the years thereafter as a veteran battling vivid memories of death and war. He believed the Lord had brought him home for a reason.

Nearly three years later, on April 3, 2003, the Lord took my dad home to heaven. Today he lies buried in a hillside grave overlooking miles of farm fields. He is, at last, no longer tormented by the horrors of war, but forever at peace with the Father who brought him safely home.

⌣ *My Grace Is Sufficient* ⌣

NELDA JONES, EDGEWOOD, TEXAS

BULLETS WHIZZED OVER THE HEAD of the young soldier as he crouched on the ground, slowly and carefully inching his way through the field of grain, trying to dodge the bullets spraying across the field from the enemy guns. Occasionally he felt and heard the ping of bullets hitting his army helmet.

Jimmy Allen was no stranger to grain fields, having been reared on small farms and in rural communities of Texas. However, he never thought he would be dodging bullets in one, especially in faraway France. It was 1918, during World War I, and Jimmy had been sent to fight with the allied troops. *What is going to become of me?* he wondered. *Am I going to die here, so far away from home, without ever seeing my parents and family again? And what about Effie, the sweet young lady I had left behind in Texas?*

He hoped she would be waiting for him. He had not felt that it would be right to ask her to wait, since he had no idea how long it would be before he returned…or even if he would return. *Will I ever have a chance to tell Effie how I feel about her and ask her to be my wife?* he wondered as he continued to make his way across the field in the crossfire of bullets, praying as he went.

As he prayed, he sensed the comforting presence of God, and a still small voice spoke to his spirit, "My grace is sufficient for thee, my son, my grace is sufficient." He recognized this as a scripture and the words of a song, which before had meant very little to him. Now the words took on a new meaning. He knew whatever might happen to him, God was with him, looking after him, and no matter what happened, God's grace truly would be sufficient.

Back in Texas, the young lady of Jimmy's dreams was growing anxious. She had not had a letter or heard any word from him in a long time. *Maybe I can get Papa to take me over to visit with Jimmy's parents,* she thought. *Maybe they've heard something since we last talked to them.*

She could hardly sleep as she tossed and turned in bed. "Father, is he all right? Why have we not heard from him? Father, please take care of Jimmy for me and bring him safely home." As she prayed quietly, she felt God's presence as He spoke to her spirit, reassuring her. "Don't worry about him anymore. He's going to be all right. I will take care of him." Then she drifted off to sleep peacefully, knowing God would keep His promise.

However, when her parents took her to visit with Jimmy's parents, she was disappointed to find out they had not heard anything either. In fact, it would be quite a while before they would hear anything about the events that were transpiring in France.

Jimmy had been captured by the Germans, along with many other French and American soldiers, in the Battle of Chateau Thierry. They were packed like cattle in boxcars and had to stand for hours during the long, grueling train trip across the country to a German prison camp.

Being a farmer was in his favor, for soon after he was captured he was sent to live and work on a German farm, raising potatoes that were probably being sent to feed the German troops or other prisoners—or both. The family who owned the farm treated him well and was just as happy and excited as he when they received word the war was finally over.

There was just as much excitement in both Jimmy and Effie's families when they received word he was finally coming home. In the spring of 1919, both families went to the train station to welcome him. In June of that year Jimmy and Effie were married.

God's grace truly had been sufficient. Jimmy brought home proof of God's grace and protection. The helmet he had been wearing that day in the grain field bore witness to that fact. There were several dents in the steel helmet where the bullets had hit. One had actually pierced the steel, yet he was unhurt.

Yes, God's grace protected my father on the battlefield that day, kept him through several months as a prisoner of war, and brought him safely home to my mother. God's grace also kept him and his family through many years ahead as they reared twelve children on a small Texas farm.

Dad lived to be ninety-nine years old, and even in his late nineties, his voice would still choke up with tears when he would recall the day God spoke those comforting words to him, "My grace is sufficient for thee." It was God's truth that empowered his life from that point forward—and because he had become a changed man at that moment, he changed all of our lives as a father who believed in the power of prayer.

~ *Lesson from Desert Storm* ~

Dr. Danny Smith, as told to Kayleen Reusser, Bluffton, Indiana

A succession of deafening explosions ripped through the night and woke me from a fitful sleep. I immediately put on my gas mask and bolted from my cot to join other personnel who had gathered at the barrack's windows. Black smoke and flying debris obliterated our view of the war-torn Kuwaiti desert. The cacophony of noise sounded different from the other times we'd been fired at by one of Saddam Hussein's low-flying Soviet Scud missiles. Later we learned that a seventeen-foot Allied rocket, the Patriot, had broken the sound barrier and blown away an incoming Scud in a fiery collision. It was history's first wartime intercept of a ballistic missile. A television crew on the roof of a nearby building caught the event on film. Millions of American viewers watched it at home.

I was platoon commander of the Army National Guard medical unit stationed out of Iowa City, Iowa. Our unit had been deployed to Kuwait in January 1991, as part of a massive military buildup by the United States to combat Saddam Hussein's invasion of Kuwait. Our mission was to perform advance trauma life support, stabilize the wounded, and send them back to the MASH unit or field hospital in the rear. Medical intelligence told us that due to an increase in air strikes, we should expect 500 to 1000 casualties a day. The news, the heat, the stress of waiting, and our proximity to danger created a palpable tension within camp. It was my duty to maintain order. Thus far I had done so, but I wondered how long it would last.

As a Christian, I often sought help from the Scriptures. Psalm 91, in particular, gave me strength and courage. Verse three could refer to biological and chemical warfare: "Surely he will save you…from the deadly pestilence." Verse five says, "You will not fear the terror of night." I took that to mean the Scud missile attacks. The words, written thousands of years ago, seemed to fit our twentieth-century situation amazingly well and never failed to give me assurance that God was in control.

I had always believed that everyone dealt with God in his or her own way, and I never forced my faith on anyone. As the days passed, however, tension grew and I questioned my motives. Was I keeping silent about my faith out of concern for others or because I was afraid of what others would think? That night I was ashamed to realize it was the latter, and I prayed for wisdom.

The next day, Bible in hand, I ordered the entire platoon to assemble in the mess hall. "No one knows when this thing will end or if any of us will walk away from it. I've been scared, and I think most of you have been scared too. But I believe Someone greater than Saddam is watching over us right now. It's someone who cares what happens to us. God, our Creator, loves us and is able to protect us." Then I read the 16 verses of Psalm 91.

They were so familiar I could have read them with my eyes closed. That day, however, they took on new meaning as my voice rang with conviction, "He who dwells in the shelter of the Most High will abide in the shadow of the Almighty..." (NASB). Afterward, I said a short prayer and dismissed the platoon. Several people thanked me for reading the Scripture, and the next day I noticed soldiers reading the New Testaments issued to them. Something had changed—and it was good.

Two days later, when 160 of us were sent up to the front line to support the 3rd Artillery Division from 7th Corps out of Europe, I understood the power of God's Word. We were dug into our bunkers, two kilometers behind the Iraqi–Saudi border. The 100-hour Ground War began. Our unit had casualties, but they were mostly minor shrapnel injuries. We never had the hundreds of battle-related casualties that medical intelligence predicted. When the Allied forces called a truce with Saddam, we praised God that our entire unit had escaped with little injury. A few weeks later, our platoon returned to the States.

After a warm reception from my family and a period of rest, I resumed my private medical practice. On the surface, my life appeared to be the same as it was before the Gulf War...but it wasn't. I had begun to pray with patients who were having a tough time. I shared the things God was doing in my life with colleagues. When a doctor friend left the States to begin missionary work in Africa, I read Psalm 91 at his going-away party.

As soon as I stopped being silent about my faith, God began to answer my prayers in powerful ways. The Gulf War was a difficult time of separation for my family. If, however, I was given the opportunity to serve my country overseas again, I would. I believe in the ideals this country stands for, and I believe that God's plan is far greater than any I could ever imagine.

Today my faith is an active part of my life, and I can't help but wonder if that would be true had I not served in the Gulf War. I'll probably never have the answer to that question this side of heaven—but still I wonder. And still I lift my eyes for answers.

◡﹕ *Mail from Mosul* ﹕◡

JEAN WISE, EDON, OHIO

JANUARY 15, 2005

Dear Emily,

I hope you are doing well. I counted down the New Year waiting for my flight out of Baghdad and up to northern Iraq. That's right. In less than two days, our entire camp packed up, and we flew back up to Mosul.

Mosul has become the key battleground area in Iraq right now. The media liked to use that phrase "battleground" to describe states like Ohio and Pennsylvania during the U.S. election. Well, up here, the "campaign" is of a slightly higher caliber.

This is our second trip to Mosul. When we arrived in Mosul the last time, most of the schools were in shambles. The Iraqi government had neglected them for more than fifteen years. Criminals looted them during the war and stole anything of even slight value.

We worked hard to rebuild the only boys high school in the area. We restored the running water, rebuilt the bathrooms, replastered and painted the walls, and planted a garden. We created soccer fields and basketball courts. We replaced broken windows and fitted the new ones with mosquito netting. We provided new blackboards, set up a computer lab, and gave the teachers furniture and supplies. One teacher told us we created a paradise out of a hell.

This day, I thought, *is going to mark a new beginning for Mosul children and teachers.*

Since the school was in our battalion sector, the commander wanted to come for the dedication. He planned to arrive at 9:30 AM, and we would form a convoy out to the school for the 10 AM ceremony. We had our vehicles lined up at 9:15, just waiting, when we heard an explosion powerful enough to rattle our windows. A few seconds later, the sound of small arms fire filled the air. Then the radios in our vehicles started to go hot. The commander was under attack. That was all we needed to hear.

Within seconds our vehicles were rolling toward the gunfire. We had our weapons on red, locked, and loaded. We rolled into his location as the last burst of rounds filled the air. We secured the position and found our way to the commander to find out what had happened. What we saw broke our hearts.

The commander was leading a three-vehicle convoy. His vehicle passed a construction ditch in the road that was covered up with dirt. As the second Humvee passed over the ditch, it tripped an IED (improvised explosive device). The force of the explosion destroyed the vehicle and blew the leg off the young specialist who was driving.

A sergeant from the first vehicle managed to get to the wounded soldier, moving toward him under fire and applying first aid. As he placed a lifesaving tourniquet around the specialist's severed leg, we arrived to secure the area. Medics quickly evacuated the young soldier to the hospital. I removed his foot with the boot still on it from the vehicle. It could only have been God's protection no one died and only one was severely injured.

As we began our gruesome task of cleaning up, the sacrifices America asks of its young service members rose in our minds. No one said a word, and although I'm the chaplain and it's up to me to offer lessons in times like these, all I could think of was "Duty–Honor–Country."

While some days are better than others and the news media sensationalizes the casualties, please remember there is an incredible amount of good being done for the Iraqi public. Good things largely being ignored by the media. About a week after we arrived back in Mosul the second time, we revisited the school. We were thrilled to watch the kids play a soccer game on the field we built. The teachers kept thanking and thanking us. The school is thriving and educating the future of Iraq.

Thanks so much for the packages and for the kind words. It is a great feeling to know you care about us and support us over here. Just want you to know God has protected many others and me over here. Please keep praying for our safety and protection. Our Battalion Commander has pointed out every day the numerous "close calls" many of our guys have had. This is not just luck, but truly a direct result of the protection from your prayers. We have had some guys wounded, but thankfully no one has been banged up too badly.

The other day one of our guys was shot in the head. Amazingly, the bullet went through his helmet, banged around inside above his head and finally came to a stop under his scalp. The doctor pulled the bullet out and gave him a couple stitches. I saw him the next day, and he had a bandage over the back of his head. He said other than a bad headache, he felt great. The next day he was back with his platoon.

I think our Battalion Commander has counted over a dozen instances of divine intervention, and those are just the blatantly obvious ones. Just today we had another guy take a bullet to the head. He is fine and says he has a bad headache and needs a new helmet.

There was one particular time when forty enemy personnel ambushed us. Outnumbered, we all escaped without any major injuries. There have been many other stories—occasions when grenades never blew up or bounced off the ground, mortars landing next to someone yet they wouldn't receive a scratch, or soldiers who actually saw bullets going around other soldiers.

One of the guys from my company showed me the book of Nahum this evening. I must admit I've studied very little about Nahum. In Nahum, God speaks about the city of Nineveh and would you believe Mosul is built on and around ancient Nineveh? In fact, the locals say that Jonah is buried in the middle of the city. Nahum 1:7-8 states, "The LORD is good, a refuge in times of trouble. He cares for those who trust in him, but with an overwhelming flood he will make an end of Nineveh." I am sure Nahum was not referring to the present, but a flood of war has definitely come to this city. Nahum's description of Nineveh is full of violence and destruction, but I will continue to cling to his message of comfort in verse 7: "The LORD is good, a refuge in times of trouble."

Recently I found myself reflecting on the past nine months, particularly how privileged I am to be an American citizen. When I eat in the chow tent, I realize how much better I am eating than the citizens of Iraq. There I am, surrounded by enemies, enjoying a better standard of living than those outside the perimeter.

Somehow, I feel God is part of all of this, at least in helping me to trust Him more. God definitely has sent His angels to protect us. So thank you again for the letters, packages, and especially for all of your prayers. Our unit goes home soon. Can't wait!

Your friend in Iraq,

Dan

∾ *Daily Prayers for Survival* ∾

Norman "Dutch" Holland, Retired Army Colonel,
Huntsville, Alabama, as told to Jennifer Devlin

I am a Christian, baptized with my father and brother when I was a young man, and I know the power of prayer. My family continually prayed for my three brothers and me while we were fighting for freedom in World War II, and I know God heard those prayers each and every day. All four of us came home safely. My sweet wife also covered me in prayer, and I am forever grateful. One of our chaplains continually encouraged us to pray for our families back home, and I did. I prayed daily God would allow me to survive the war, and I would get safely home.

During my service in World War II, there were many instances I knew God's hand of protection was on my life and the lives of the men who served alongside me. There were many times during the war that God spared me from death during times of battle.

Early in the war, my unit was a member of the beachhead landing in southern Sicily, July 1943. Since it was new to all of us (we had no previous battle experience), a ship-wide prayer was offered: "Lord, we don't know what is ahead of us, but we know You go before us at all times, and at this time, we pray Your hand of protection will be on us."

On landing that early morning, the enemy began their artillery attack, forcing us to dig foxholes on the beach with our helmets and then with our hands. An 88mm shell landed amid our spread-out unit. We lay flat in shallow foxholes until the incoming shelling abated. In reviewing the results, I am convinced it was a "Godsend" that the German shells were not equipped with extended fuses. As a result, the shells penetrated far enough into the sand, prior to exploding, so that the lateral fragmentation stayed within the sand and did not harm our troops.

Later in the day, after reaching our temporary bivouac area, I had to travel to our headquarters twice. First, had I taken a short-cut path instead of staying on the longer road, I might have been killed. I learned later the path was booby-trapped; unknowingly, each trip took me past an Italian machine gun nest, which could have taken my life. God again protected me.

On the second day at the beachhead, the Germans increased their attacks, including air attacks. One "skip" bomber, aiming for our ship, was hit. Trying to escape, he jettisoned his heavy bomb, which landed within our bivouac area. When that bomb exploded, I was knocked unconscious for the first time in my life. When I regained consciousness, I thought someone had jumped in on me, and I yelled for them to get off. However, when I pushed myself up I realized I was covered in dirt—almost buried. Things were chaotic with individuals yelling, screaming, crying, and dashing around. I began coughing blood. When medics arrived, they quickly sent me to the aid station, where I was evacuated to a converted hospital ship and later placed in an evacuation hospital.

Upon recovery of internal injuries, I rejoined my unit in October 1943, in Italy. It was there I learned six of our men had been killed and six wounded in the battle. Two of those killed were our machinists Houston, a Protestant, and Kincaid, a Catholic. Both were devout Christians who loved and obeyed the Lord dearly. When Houston was removed from his foxhole, they found him holding his issued New Testament open, which he had been reading at the time of the bomb explosion. Then, and even now, I have prayed that God called them all home to eternal life, void of all suffering. I have often thanked God since that time that He spared the survivors to continue to live and be available to do His bidding.

Then there was the Battle for Anzio. It was only supposed to be a ten- to fifteen-day fight, but it lasted 124 days, with 67,000 casualties.

It became more profound as time went on just how God's hand of protection was with me, and how the prayers of my family covered me in battle.

I was billeted in a villa in Netuno. One day I went to check on fellow soldiers after a shelling attack. Our courier and I met Thomas, who borrowed the courier's bicycle to check out his billet. We left Thomas there on the road while he placed his pants legs into his socks to ride the bicycle. The courier and I were about twenty or thirty yards up the street and had just stepped inside a doorway when a German 280mm shell struck the building we had left just seconds before. As smoke and debris settled, I prayed aloud that Thomas had already departed. However I found him dead on the street. I prayed God had fully accepted his soul and thanked Him for sparing the lives of the courier and me. Over and over, I know the prayers that went up on my behalf helped spare my life. Prayer was as active a part of my life as breathing.

One day one of our men was squatting against an inner wall, talking with the cooks. A 280mm shell hit an Aqua Vita distillery building nearby and sent a shell fragment the size of my fist through the ceiling and roof. It ricocheted off the terrazzo floor, through the man, the wall, and was found lying on the floor in the next room. The man later died.

One night, six 50kg German bombs were dropped, and five of them landed in our location, one directly outside our area. What are the odds that the five bombs that landed in our area would be duds? Yet they were, and the sixth one exploded beyond. If they had all exploded, our entire company could have been killed. I never heard them drop because of the antiaircraft fire and noise always present during a bombing raid. But I was busy praying during the whole ordeal for God to keep us safe. I remember looking at where the bombs landed afterward, and all I could say over and over again was "thank You, God!"

Later, an explosive ordnance soldier came over to defuse one of the bombs. He used a pickaxe and shovel to get the unexploded bomb out, and I, like an idiot, was standing there watching and talking with him. At one point, the pickaxe hit the bomb, and the soldier looked up, saying, "I sure hope my girlfriend is in church right now…" We both understood the necessity for prayer.

One night, I was offered a good night's sleep in a wine cellar by one of my men because the British soldier who usually slept there had been killed. I took the offer, and in the morning, I got up and went to my usual sleeping place. Upon entering, I saw a jagged hole through the door and just above my usual bed, a jagged hole on the wall. Lying on my bed was a shell fragment, which probably would have killed me had I been in the bed. Again, I was spared. I kept that fragment for many years as a reminder of that time of protection.

Looking back on all these events, it's obvious God's protection was on me and those of my unit during my whole deployment experience. God answered the prayers of my family and wife, as they prayed my brothers and I would come back alive, which we all did. God answered my personal prayers for survival on a daily basis.

Many times I have asked, "Dear God, why wasn't it me? God, why did You choose to spare my life? What do You have in store for me?" I still don't fully know the answer to these questions, but God does. His guardian angels protected me then, and still do so today.

Apparently, He's not quite done with me yet. I pray often I shall be worthy of the long life He has loaned to me.

∽ Twilight Prayer ∾

DANIEL FAHNCKE, AS TOLD TO
SUSAN FARR FAHNCKE, KAYSVILLE, UTAH

I STARED AT THE PHOTO IN MY HANDS, faded with time and dark at the edges, since twilight had been falling at the time the picture was taken. The memories of Vietnam came flooding back. My time in Vietnam changed and shaped me in ways no other event in my life has before or since.

Vietnam was my first exposure to death, and we lived closely with it on a daily basis. I was an eighteen-year-old kid who would rather be home in the States, dragging the boulevard and just being eighteen, instead of giving the next thirteen months of my life over to being a part of a horror that those who weren't there can never fully understand. During my duty in Vietnam, I changed and became hard inside—like many of those who fought alongside me.

Even today, many of us have deadened or hardened the sore spots left over from the war in one way or another. The nightmare of the "conflict" did this to us. We learned the hardening of emotion, the withdrawal and repression of all feelings.

Freedom has a meaning to fighters that the protected will never know.

Prayer was a constant, and the one I recall most often was my plea, "Lord, get me out of here," which was often followed by, "Why Lord? Why him? Why me? Why not?" It all seemed so senseless. Yet I prayed, almost ceaselessly, during my entire time on Vietnamese soil.

The photo in my hands trembles slightly as the memories it opens splash out and wash over me. Rare were the moments that laughter or relaxation was allowed. Every waking and sleeping moment we had to be on our guard, always at the ready, prepared to kill or be killed.

At the time the photo was taken, the detail I was serving with had been holed up in the middle of a North Vietnamese-infested area. Danger was heavy in our minds and all around us. We had been fighting endless weary battles for days on end, one fading into another and another, all senseless killing that robbed us of our innocence, our youth, and our lives.

This day was a reprieve from the war. A day when it had all gotten to be too much. The line between darkness and spiritual light blurred. We needed an outlet. So we played. Like children, we laughed and splashed and allowed ourselves a day off from the hell that was Vietnam. I remember the bliss…the knots in my stomach easing for a few hours as I let myself just be eighteen for a while. The day was blessed with God's grace, and we decided to spend it just living, not surviving, but in being alive. Our laughter still echoes in memory playing back, the river calm and almost peaceful, sparkling as the sun shone down upon it, our day in the sun the best therapy—aside from going home—that we could have.

We sunbathed and for a few precious hours we were just kids letting loose. Gunfire never erupted, death never stole that moment from us, and God watched over and gave us that day. Having had a few good hours of much-needed relaxation, I was thankful for the memory and the protection of the Lord there under the shadow of death. That single day drew me closer to God in many ways.

The Twenty-third Psalm ran through my mind as the sun lowered into the horizon, and I knelt along the riverbank to thank God for our safe haven from the war.

> The LORD is my shepherd, I shall not be in want. He makes me lie down in green pastures, he leads me beside quiet waters, he restores my soul. He guides me in paths of righteousness for his name's sake. Even though I walk

through the valley of the shadow of death, I will fear no evil, for you are with me; your rod and your staff they comfort me. You prepare a table before me in the presence of my enemies. You anoint my head with oil; my cup overflows. Surely goodness and love will follow me all the days of my life, and I will dwell in the house of the LORD forever" (Psalm 23).

My buddy snapped the picture that now rests in my hands. It tells a story words cannot convey. It is twilight in Vietnam. It is the middle of a war, in the middle of enemy territory. We had survived a blissful day under God's watchful eye, and I am on the riverbank, on my knees, in grateful prayer. My twilight prayer in Vietnam.

2

Lessons Learned and Lives Changed

Ever have one of those moments when you realize God's hand has been there, and you've just come through a divine appointment? It can take your breath away to know, beyond a shadow of a doubt, that God ordered the events surrounding you with better than military precision. Be it the frustratingly late start that actually saved your life or the surprising friendship that changed your world forever, there is no question that God is in control down to even the minutest details of our existence. He has a plan for our lives, and He wants to help us be the best we can be. Sometimes it takes years before we see what God wanted us to learn from a specific event; other times, it's instantaneous realization. And, just like an earthly parent, we bring Him joy when we learn from the life lessons He sends our way. Can't you just hear God saying, "I just love it when My kids listen!"

❧❧❧

There is a time for everything,
and a season for every activity under heaven.

Ecclesiastes 3:1

✌ Each Letter Was a Prayer ✌

NANCY C. ANDERSON, HUNTINGTON BEACH, CALIFORNIA

I JUST READ ALL OF HIS LETTERS AGAIN. They help me understand the lonely losses and the vivid victories of the war—the Civil War.

My great-great-great-grandfather, Henry B. Rowe, wrote twenty-nine letters that taught me about bravery, honor, and prayerful perseverance in the face of fear. He was a Yankee farmer who wanted to preserve the Union and free the slaves, so he became a soldier—and marched south.

He kissed his wife, Lucinda, and their three young children goodbye on a chilly October day in 1864, and joined the ranks of the 18th Division of the Wisconsin Volunteers.

His letters, addressed to his wife, were poetic and filled with love and faith. He wrote: "May heaven's choicest blessings rest upon you and the children. Be true and faithful soldiers for Christ, and I will be the same for my country. And if I fall for my country, then it will be an honor to you. I pray that we may meet again where wars will never separate us."

Those letters are more significant than any history book I will ever read because a man whose blood still flows through me wrote those words. I am a writer, as he was a writer. I am a Christian because faith can also flow through families. His heritage, his legacy, was one of strength and perseverance, kindness and prayerful obedience.

His division joined the ranks of General William Tecumseh Sherman on his infamous "March to the Sea." The horrors of war were exploding around this relative of mine, and yet he loved, as Christ commanded, even his enemies.

His words from Winston, North Carolina, March 16, 1865:

Oh, you can't begin to think how the women and children suffer as we pass through. Some of the soldiers take anything, burn everything, but I will not do such work. Yesterday, I stopped at a house and there sat a woman with three children, not a thing in the world to eat. I saw that her baby girl was sick with the measles so I gave the mother my rations and passed on. She thanked me kindly with tears in her eyes…and so it goes. God speed the day that we may be a free and happy people.

His letters gave me an eyewitness account of history as it was unfolding. When he saw General Sherman, he wrote: "I saw the old chap the other day, a fine-looking man, but some care worn."

When the news of the end of the war spread though the camp, he wrote: "I heard that the Rebs surrendered from the Potomac to the Rio Grande— God grant that it may be so."

Then, regarding one of darkest days of the century, his tender words reflect his sadness. Raleigh, North Carolina, April 18, 1865: "There is a great gloom in the camp at the announcing of the murder of our President."

He thought he was only writing letters to his wife, but he was also writing to me. I'm learning who I am by reading who he was. Each letter included a prayer for peace in our country and peace in the

Henry B. Rowe, Union soldier, Civil War

hearts of his family. God answered those prayers as the war came to an end and he traveled back to his tranquil farm. He was thin and ragged, but he showed new strength as he jumped off his horse, scooped up his children, and kissed his wife.

It is my prayer today, as men and women return from the conflicts abroad, that they remember what our forefathers experienced while fighting for peace and freedom on our own soil. The conflicts may be different, but the ability to pray to a God who understands things we cannot remains the same. Whether we are on the battlefield of war or the battlefield of wondering if our loved ones will come home, we are all called to be "true and faithful soldiers for Christ."

↫ The Mourning After ↬

Rachel I. Blevins, Fredericktown, Ohio

My husband, Joe, had been home only a few days when an innocent bathroom encounter demonstrated the lingering effects war can have. He was showering when I walked in unannounced and slapped the shower curtain to let him know I was in the room.

"Don't you ever do that again!" Joe barked.

"Do what?" I asked, surprised at his tone.

"Don't you ever scare me like that again!"

I was dumbfounded. "What are you talking about?"

"Just don't surprise me like that anymore," Joe repeated.

Discharge from active service does not discharge a man from the effects of war. Freedom comes with a price tag, and full disclosure is seldom given. Sudden noises...surprises...fireworks...flashbacks...hunting...mistrust of foreigners, especially children...all these things had changed for Joe since he returned from the Vietnam War. Neither of us realized the challenges that faced us in the years ahead.

Joe no longer wanted to attend the local fireworks display on the Fourth of July. Another behavior I didn't comprehend…what's the big deal about fireworks? But Joe had been in the infantry division, and the sound of explosives was too fresh in his mind.

And children…why would he have issues with children?

But then Joe told me of how he had witnessed children who had become killing machines, to the point of even exterminating their own parents in Vietnam, as a result of communist brainwashing. He despised the way the enemy used children in its war tactics. He never thought he could distrust children, but his wariness had built up over the time he was stationed there. It took a long time before our children and grandchildren helped erase that bitterness.

A few months after Joe came home, a friend asked him to go hunting. This would be his first time back in the woods…and he hesitated, but eventually decided to go anyway, to be with his buddy. It turned out to be a terrible experience. Joe found himself looking for people instead of animals, and he jumped at the slightest movement in the woods. His former love of hunting was now just a painful memory.

In those days, there was no diagnosis of what we now know as Post Traumatic Stress Disorder. Counseling might have helped us understand what was happening. Things like flashbacks…flailing arms and groans in the middle of the night. Night sweats. What a horrible reminder of the past. We mourned the loss of our more carefree life before the war.

As a young wife I had no idea what to do or how to help my husband overcome these things except to pray. As time passed, more and more things bothered him. Even eating in an Asian restaurant was disconcerting. He rarely talked about his struggles, preferring to suffer in silence. At that time he had a job as a salesman, but I later discovered he just couldn't do his job some days. How do you explain to the boss that you cannot concentrate...or have no motivation to work? I continued to pray that he would be healed of the awful memories.

One time we traveled out of the country to the Cayman Islands to visit family. I noticed that he seemed upset soon after we arrived. "What's the problem?" I asked. "I just don't get it. Is it the driving on the left side of the road? Is it the sea? What is bothering you?"

"I'll be glad when we go home," Joe said. "I don't like being in a foreign country...not after being in Vietnam."

"Well, this is hardly like Vietnam," I answered. "You know people here. My brother is here. And they do speak English, even though the natives speak in a different rhythm than you're used to. Please, try to calm down." I'm afraid I was insensitive because I simply did not understand.

Neither of us realized how uncomfortable Joe would be on this tropical island. How would he ever overcome this unwarranted suspicion? After his job in sales, he had become a pastor and regularly exhorted others to "love one another" in his messages. So why was it so difficult for him in these situations? I continued praying the Lord would show us a way.

In 2004, Joe consented to go to Port-au-Prince, Haiti, on a short missions trip. He knew he would be faced with cultural differences and a foreign language barrier. Again we prayed that God would give him the grace to face this new challenge.

The terrain was very similar to that of Vietnam, including the tall sugar cane fields that looked like the elephant grass of Southeast Asia. Haitians would emerge from the cane fields and remind Joe of the Viet Cong exiting the elephant grass. So many reminders...

But a wonderful transformation took place while Joe was in Haiti. The children stole his heart as he watched them carry heavy loads on their small bodies...as some sat outside a school to listen and learn because there was no room for them inside and no money to attend...as they rode through the city in the back of a truck and sang songs of joy. God changed Joe's heart and gave him a love for these foreigners and their land. Almost overnight he had been healed.

What made the difference? Time? Another country? Perhaps, but we believe it was prayer and preparation that changed his heart. We believe the power of prayer can change a life.

The flashbacks rarely occur now. Joe does not spook easily, but hunting is still off limits…and that's okay with him.

But memories resurface after the occasional flashback…standing beside a statue of soldiers…viewing a granite wall of 58,220 names… military cemeteries…fireworks displays on the Fourth of July…a veteran standing at attention as Old Glory passes by in the home-town parade. These are things that will forever remind my husband of a time long ago, in a place far away.

We have learned not to take for granted the scars involved and the mourning that comes with such life-changing events. But we don't lose heart, either, because prayer has made a difference and has lessened the aftermath of war in our lives.

Mourning has broken and joy has come. Hallelujah!

✥ *Power of Effective Prayer* ✥

MIKE WARREN, OKLAHOMA CITY, OKLAHOMA,
AND CARLO SERRANO, FORT CAMPBELL, KENTUCKY

"GOD, PROTECT MY FAMILY IN MY ABSENCE, watch over me during this deployment, and please do not allow me to become ineffective in my spiritual endeavors." This prayer was first spoken while in flight from Fort Campbell, Kentucky, home of the 101st Airborne Division (Air Assault) to Kuwait, and it was repeated many times thereafter during my seven-month tour. I had left behind a pregnant wife, with our third child due on April 26, and was headed for yet another "desert experience."

On March 1, 2003, my unit landed in Kuwait to prepare for the next step in our country's war on terrorism. We stayed in Kuwait for nearly a month, waiting and preparing for the inevitable. We spent most of our time training for our mission, but too often spent much more of it missing home. My wife continued to attend the Protestant Women of the Chapel (PWOC) at Fort Campbell, while I searched for some Christian involvement in the ancient land of our spiritual ancestors. There were infrequent chapel services, which were difficult to attend because of the variety of schedules we soldiers lived, so I opted to recruit what Christians I could find to a Bible study devoted to finding out how God would train us to accomplish His will.

Ken Conklin and Frank Molisee were the first two young disciples I found willing to help me grow in my faith. I shared with them what I had learned from ten years of discipleship training. I told them, "If you want to build a strong foundation that will stand the tests of war and peace, you must stay on top of spiritual disciplines like quiet times, Scripture memory, Bible study, and fellowship, and above all, you must not quit."

In April, we advanced into Iraq. Our spiritual disciplines were temporarily overshadowed by the disciplines of war as we fought to bring peace where violence had always been prevalent. Prayer was our calling, and hope for safety was our burden. By mid-April, we arrived in Mosul, Iraq, and began operations that would last until the 101st left in March of the following year. While there Ken, Frank, and I started a weekly Bible study, and two other believers joined us regularly, Chris Moore and Carlo Serrano.

"The worse thing about the Mosul airport was the smell," Carlo told me, as we later remembered our shared experiences over lunch one day at Fort Campbell. "The raw sewage, the Tigris River, and the sugar factory across the street made breathing barely tolerable. An added strain was the realization that I had just abandoned my eight-month pregnant wife and three-year-old son to serve my country in a land I had only seen on a map. I was two months into the wildest emotional ride of my life.

"On my first day in Kuwait, I received news that my wife had lost the babies she was carrying." Carlo's tears were unwilling to escape the capture of his eyes during his retelling, but they never clouded his vision of the hope that was his strength. Carlo then reminded me of our divine appointment.

"I knew God wanted me to learn from this trial, and He wanted me here in Mosul for a reason. Then I saw you sitting in the corner of the airport terminal with about six other soldiers, studying the Word of God. My heart leapt as I realized the purpose for my presence. I had treasured His Word since I left the U.S., and my faith was really all that kept me sane during my trials. Yet I knew God had more for me than just reading my Bible. I knew He had called me to serve Him and lead others to do the same. That's when I met you."

Carlo recalled our meeting as though it had been yesterday. "The first time we talked one on one, you turned my personal theology upside down, and over the next couple of months you never ceased to challenge my faith. You told me to read the Bible every day, to pray without ceasing, to share Jesus without fear, to hide His Word in my heart through memorization, and to meet with other believers as if my life depended on it. I thought you were nuts, but I did it anyway. And when I faltered, you said, 'Don't quit. God has called you to Himself for such a time as this.'"

I thank God I was able to help Carlo on his journey.

By the end of April, my new daughter, Abigail Faith Warren, was born. I had hoped for a chance to fly home and be present for her birth, but this blessing was not afforded me. Once the end of the war was announced, I prayed for a ticket home, but instead received a new mission. My task was simple. Lead a convoy of soldiers into the city of Mosul, find schools that needed repair, hire local contractors to accomplish the work, and oversee the completion of the rebuilding.

As you might imagine, this mission wasn't safe, but God protected us. On one trip we were in downtown Mosul, shopping for school supplies, when suddenly we heard the familiar cracking of automatic fire. We quickly returned to our vehicles and saw a large crowd of angry faces massing together like dark clouds. We loaded our vehicles for an impromptu escape, but were frightened when one Humvee wouldn't start. We spent what seemed an eternity cranking the engine as we attempted to jump the battery from another vehicle. In the distance we could clearly see men with AK47s firing into the crowds. Fortunately, they hadn't seen us or didn't want to involve us. Either way, we knew we had to leave. We piled into the remaining vehicles and left the disabled one for the crowds. Moments later it was in flames, but we were safe.

As terrifying as this situation was, I do not believe it was fear that became the voice of doubt in my heart. It was

Carlo Serrano—"Do not give up. God will strengthen you as you put your trust in Him."

thoughts of home, where a new child I had never seen was looking for her father. The sound of my children's voices on the phone asking when I would come home caused me unbearable pain, while thoughts of home imprisoned all my time. I felt my prayers were ineffective and started to wonder if God was really with me. And just as God placed me in his path when he needed help the most, there was my friend Carlo, ready to lift me up.

Through tear-filled eyes Carlo told me, "Do not give up. God will strengthen you as you put your trust in Him."

I believe we both found His purpose for our deployment those long months we spent together away from home. We found His promises were true, faith is evidenced when it is tried, and we were far stronger when we shared our struggles than if we kept them tied up in the strongbox of our inward sorrows.

Today, thousands of miles away from the desert I once called home, I daily pray the promise of Isaiah 43:4 and ask that God might help me be effective for Him. My friend Carlo does the same.

> Since you are precious and honored in my sight, and because I love you, I will give men in exchange for you, and people in exchange for your life (Isaiah 43:4).

❦ The Prayer Card ❧

CHARLOTTE ADELSPERGER, OVERLAND PARK, KANSAS

DAY AFTER DAY, FOR MANY WEEKS, Joe, age twenty-two, agonized through grueling challenges at Army boot camp in Fort Knox,

Kentucky. Even though proud to be in the United States military, he was sometimes so exhausted he wondered if he'd make it through training. He drew on his closeness to God through prayer, savored his mother's letters, and dreamed of marrying his sweetheart, Tara.

His mom, Suzy, often responded to the discouragement in his letters with "Be strong in the Lord" or "Go for the gold—you can do it."

One day Joe wrote about how the men all lined up and were each assigned a partner or "battle buddy." "We need to know everything about our buddy down to his shoe size," he commented. "We're trained to look after each other wherever we go."

Joe liked his assigned buddy, Anthony, right off. They began to share everything and cheer each other on. Both were Christians. Many nights throughout boot camp some of the guys would gather in the barracks for prayer and sharing. Joe and Anthony, with their Bibles in hand, would lead the group.

One day Anthony received a worn-out prayer card in the mail from his mother. On one side was a line drawing of the head and shoulders of Jesus. His likeness emitted strength and hope. On the other side was a simple prayer for protection. His mom had written in her note, "You pray this prayer, and God will get you through anything." Anthony began using it with the group almost every night.

Sometimes when the group was feeling down, Anthony would hold up the card and say something like, "Come on, guys, we can make it through. We've got the good Lord watching our backs."

Joe remembered those words and treasured each evening with the group. He lived close to God, deeply cared about others, and saw service to his country as one of God's callings.

When Joe's parents, Mike and Suzy, attended his graduation from boot camp, Joe took them to meet Anthony. "This is my battle buddy—you've got to meet him!" Suzy gave Anthony a big hug. "I've heard what a special friend you are. I'm so glad you guys were here for each other." Mike smiled as he shook Anthony's hand.

But sadness hovered over the two buddies who had become like brothers. Anthony would be leaving for more Army training in Fort Bliss, Texas. Joe would go to Fort Hood, Texas, for training to be a cavalry scout.

"Well, we knew one day we'd be separated," Anthony said, looking into Joe's eyes. "But it looks like we're both eventually going to the Middle East." His eyes moistened as he reached into his pocket. "The prayer card is yours now. I want you to have it." He slipped it into Joe's hand.

"Thanks," Joe said, looking down at the card. He shuffled his feet, and then pointed to the picture. "One day, that'll be a tattoo on my back!" Everyone chuckled.

During his ten-day leave, Joe and Tara made a life commitment and were married. It was then, before going to Fort Hood, that Joe made another life commitment.

"Mom, I have to show you something." He pulled off his shirt. A thin plastic covering clung to his slim back. When she saw traces of blood across his dark skin, a chill swept over her. There beneath the plastic bandage was the very sketch of Jesus that had been on the prayer card—about six inches high, between the shoulder blades of her son.

"Oh, my word! You really did it." She fought tears as she pictured Joe, with this image on his back, on the front lines of a battlefield.

"You don't get a tattoo just for the fun of it," he said. "I prayed about this one. Now wherever I go in life, it'll be a reminder of who's with me."

Weeks later Private First Class Joe, a recipient of honors, was deployed with U.S. Army troops to the Middle East, where he valiantly served on the front lines during Operation Iraqi Freedom.

But before Joe left, he wrote his mom. "You know, when guys see Jesus right there on my skin, I tell 'em, 'The Lord's watching my back—and yours, too.' It helps us all be stronger."

❧ ❧ ❧

∾ Out of the Mud and Mire ∾

JERRY THOMAS, UNION CITY, TENNESSEE

I WAS A PILOT IN THE UNITED STATES AIR FORCE for twenty-two years, primarily in two-engine and four-engine planes. From my earliest training days, going to Vietnam three times, flying over the Arctic Circle, and over the deserts, I always had a fear of death and "the Judgment." I attended church, but I had never truly committed my life and heart to Jesus Christ.

I have many memories of getting into serious situations that I knew I could not, by myself, get out of alive. Flying in the mountains during the night and heavy weather with communication or navigation problems, sometimes with passengers and sometimes with hazardous cargo, I would pray and cry out to God to help me. He always did; hence, I'm still here.

During those years, I flew for generals, ambassadors, admirals, and State Department officials. I flew into combat areas, with guns slinging bullets at me, or tried to land on unprepared landing strips, mountainsides, roadways, areas littered with empty shell casings, animals, beat-up vehicles, and mud...and many others situations that seemed impossible to survive. I would pray and cry out "God save me"...and He always did. But I would go right back to my old ways, generally without Him (till the next time I badly needed Him!).

Once, while flying a C-130 Hercules (four-engine cargo plane) in Vietnam, which was built to transport sixty combat troops, I was directed to carry 220 people to a mountainside dirt strip near the Laotian border. I found the strip, but a crippled plane on the end of the strip made it necessary for me to land going down the mountain. I had to drag the plane's belly through the treetops and force the plane onto the grass, gravel, and dust. While on the landing roll out, with four propellers in reverse and thrust kicking up dust so dense I could not see forward, I had to rely on the compass to steer the plane straight ahead. Again, I "reasoned" with the Lord to please save us...He did...and once again I went back to my old ways. It was a vicious circle.

I survived countless close calls in both military and civilian aircraft, but it was forty some years before I had a life-changing encounter with my Creator, and the Holy Spirit opened my eyes to at last see the pit I was in.

God had continually come to my rescue, and, while I continually called out to Him for help and thanked Him for saving me, I would continually return to my old way of life. Not until I asked the Lord to change my heart and life *forever* was I truly free. When I called on Jesus to pull me out of the pit I was in once and for all, He heard my cry...and this time I was ready to hear Him.

He showed me countless scriptures that enriched my life, and He set my feet on a rock and gave me a firm place to stand. I now see in retrospective wisdom that God answered all my prayers for help during the years because He had a plan for me.

Since then I have established a Bible study, open to the public, in my hometown. Many people have come to know the Lord and have been saved, filled with the Spirit of God to live fruitful lives. I'm a Gideon, a church member, and try to be a witness daily. With quiet daily devotions, I try to be armed with the Sword of the Spirit in order to meet the adversary with the "whole armor of God."

My wife of forty-nine years and I live a quiet life on a few acres in Tennessee. We have three children—one is a minister—and eight church-going grandchildren—we are so blessed. Thanks to the Lord, who answered the prayers of a "part-time" believer, so he could become a "full-time" witness.

❧ ❧ ❧

◡ *Jesus Loves You* ◡

G.E. DABBS, CALERA, ALABAMA

I<small>T WAS</small> J<small>ANUARY</small> 1976. I was new to the U.S. Army, a private, and had a lot of growing up to do. I was stationed in Germany at the time, and God used this event to grow His love in my heart.

Eight of us soldiers were headed to Nuremburg to hear missionary Donald (Dwayne) Duck preach the gospel at an outreach service. He didn't preach denomination, but the true gospel, the Word of God. Christians from all backgrounds were going to hear him that night, including me, a Baptist.

While we waited for our train, a bum or drunk, or possibly just a man of great suffering and deprivation due to alcohol, walked into the station. He stumbled over to the wall and leaned on it, trying to keep his balance. After propping himself, he slumped into a pile on the floor, as though he had passed out. I watched as everyone, including myself, continued going about his business, acting like this was an everyday occurrence. My buddy, George Larke, came back to us with the tickets and asked why the man was lying on the floor. He indicated concern and, being our group's preacher-type leader, he suggested that we do the Christian thing and help this man.

The eight of us surrounded him, and, using his trench coat to move him, we gently lifted him and placed him as comfortably as we could on a bench nearby. While we were carrying him, we noticed his chest under his shirt. He was bandaged as though he had broken ribs. We set him down as gently as possible, but he awoke in terrible pain. He gripped his chest and screamed in agony.

We didn't know if we were the cause of his suffering by moving him or if he had reinjured himself when he dropped to the floor. One thing we did know, however. He was in horrible pain and was having difficulty breathing. We feared he was dying and felt we may have been responsible in some way and needed to do something.

We asked the cashier to call for an ambulance while the man continued crying out. We thought he was going to slip away before the ambulance could get there. We felt we should do something, but didn't know what.

George spoke up. "Let's pray for him."

Each of us knelt down, surrounding the man, laying hands on him and prayed. Private Galloway, a believer for only three days said these words to the man. "Yesus liebt dich. Yesus, Yesus, Yesus." Jesus loves you, Jesus, Jesus, Jesus—in German.

The suffering man opened his eyes and stared at Galloway, soaking in the words. A great calm filled him even though he was still in pain. Tears filled his eyes in a new way, tears of joy. I glanced around the room and saw not only eight GIs praying, but was surprised to see every man, woman, and child at the train station kneeling and praying for this man. German nationalists and tourists alike knelt together with us, praying for a man they had earlier pitied, including myself.

Finally the ambulance arrived. The medics lifted the man as we had, placing him on the gurney to be moved to the vehicle. We followed them into the cold and watched them place him in the ambulance. I'll never forget the sight. The man outstretched his hand in gratitude, and I'll never forget that we, as Christians, can so easily touch those around us with God's love. We just have to set aside our opinionated viewpoints and get our hands dirty. Jesus can do great things when His servants go forward in faith.

That afternoon we caught our train to Nuremberg, feeling we should have gone to the hospital, but we didn't even know the man's name. Our hearts went out to a stranger whose life was touched by a group of guys who could barely speak his language. But his hope was in Christ, not in the GIs he had encountered in the train station. He recognized Jesus there, and I knew he would never be the same.

Others saw Christ too. Before the ambulance arrived, there were at least thirty people kneeling in prayer, lifting this man before God. Those who were obedient to kneel influenced those around them to join with us.

Being a witness for Christ is never easy, but Christ, through us, can do all things. I hope I will meet that man in my Father's house someday, to sit down with him and recall what God did through a few American Army men who cared...and prayed.

ॐ ॐ ॐ

↣ God's Word a Reality ↢

Major General Jim Pillsbury, Redstone Arsenal, Alabama,
as told to Jennifer Devlin

My wife and I were baptized together in a small church in Virginia in 1979. I was already an active duty officer at the time, and it was a leap of faith for both of us. We remember this time sweetly, and although it was the first step in a lifelong journey of faith, it changed our lives for eternity.

At the time I knew in my heart I was making the right decision—to follow Christ. Somehow though, it wasn't solidified in my mind. It was for the right reasons, and I knew what the words meant, but I longed for the Bible and my relationship with God to become real to me. I wanted that head/heart connection. I began praying God would reveal His Word to me in a deeply personal way. I wanted to know Him and the Bible, better. I prayed the Bible would come to life and be more real. The answer to this prayer did not come instantly, but has gradually been revealed to me over the years. I pray these revelations will continue to occur until I go to be with Him in heaven.

Back in 1979, my prayer for a deeper relationship with God was still new, and my faith was still very fresh. Life kept pressing along, and my career continued to take me to unexpected places. In 1982 and 1983, I was assigned to the Multinational Force and Observers in the Sinai, with the 101st Airborne Division rotation. This was the second military rotation to experience life on the Sinai Peninsula, and we were entrenched in providing peacekeeping operations between Israel and Egypt.

Since I was working with helicopter maintenance and was a pilot, I had a chance to see the area from a different perspective than most. We flew regular flights from the north camp to the south, which took about one-and-a-half hours each way. At about 5000 feet, the terrain looks more monotonous than on the ground, if that is possible. All you see for miles and miles is sand, a vast blanket of brown and tan covering everything below, with nothing else to look at as you fly.

During one of these trips, I studied the terrain, really thinking about the area we were in. This was the geographical area of the Bible, and I again asked God to make His Word more real to me. As I flew over the vast nothingness below, I looked in the distance and saw something very out of place. Beyond our approved flying path, I saw what looked like a lush green patch of heaven—right in the middle of the sea of dust. Was this a mirage? I flew along the outermost rim of our approved flight path to see it as closely as I could. Sure enough, there was the most green, lush patch of ground I have ever seen. It was surrounded by the vastness of the desert. It stood alone. I knew I had to find out what this could be.

I landed on base, and after finishing with my duties, I went to find out what God's Word had to say. The Bible clearly talked about a time when Moses hit a rock and water flowed from it. I read Exodus 17:6 and the image passed my eyes again, "I will stand there before you by the rock of Horeb. Strike the rock, and water will come out of it for the people to drink."

Could this be what I saw? Was this God's gift to me?

I continued searching for information about the area I had seen, and eventually I received confirmation about my experience. Indeed, that is where Moses hit the rock—and to this day, water flows there. In a dry land, there was a place that would forever quench thirst. In a dry land, we also have a place to quench our thirst. God made this experience so real. The Bible literally came alive in front of me.

Once I saw how God so wonderfully answered my prayer for really knowing the Bible more clearly, I wasn't as surprised when it happened a second time. During this same rotation in the Sinai, from time to time a bunch of us were able to go sightseeing. We took tours through Jerusalem and throughout Israel. We saw many great historic sites, and we realized how life in this region of the world was so different from the military life we lived.

One time we were even able to watch the sunrise while on top of Mount Sinai. We went to a Greek Orthodox monastery that has sat at the base of the mountain since around 600 AD and prepared for our trek. No special planning, just a bunch of "thirty-somethings" in jeans and tennis shoes geared up for a journey up a Bedouin path. I don't think any of us realized it would take well over two hours to navigate the path, nor that the monks had built a stairway—and it was over 3750 steps.

"Lord, is this really *the* mountain? Is this the place I have read about? Moses was here…thank You, Lord…" I reflected a bit about what I knew of this area. Once again, God's Word came alive for me.

Watching the sun begin to rise over the Gulf of Aqaba off the Arabian Peninsula, I was replaying the story in my mind. Here was Moses, up on the mountain with God…when God asks him to go back down and talk with the people. All I could think of was that trek. Of course, Moses didn't want to go back down there—the steps weren't even made back then. He would have to make the journey without the help of a beaten path. Moses tried his best negotiating skills, but to no avail. Off he went back down that mountain to speak to God's people. It was hard not to see the image of Moses working his way up and down that mountain as I took in the beauty of that sunrise. God indeed made His Word real to me, and my prayer was once again answered. It was an adventure none of us would ever forget. This was a truly special moment. Had I not been in the military, assigned to the Sinai, it never would have occurred.

Many times since that rotation I have thought of my time there and my request for clarity. I am amazed at how God chose to answer the prayer of my heart—to grow closer to Him by allowing me experiences through the military that I otherwise would never have had.

I still yearn to learn more about God. I know it is hard to live this life of faith, day in and day out. But every new day brings a new chance to try. Every man has a choice, and my prayer is that every man will choose God's way.

∽ When God Says No ∾

STEVEN WICKSTROM, AIEA, HAWAII

HAVE YOU EVER PRAYED TO GOD and had Him answer you by saying "no"? It's disappointing, isn't it? Sometimes we don't even know how to deal with that answer, especially when it concerns the life of a loved one. When God gives us a "no" answer, He usually doesn't explain why He answers in that way—and that makes it even more difficult to accept. God seems to expect us to accept the answer and move on. The trouble is that we often don't want to accept that answer, and we don't want to move on until we get an answer we want.

I was on a Coast Guard cutter in the Bering Sea in the middle of February. The relentless storms had driven the waves to twenty feet, and the snow was coming down horizontally. Being on a ship in rough seas is absolutely uncomfortable. Every morning we had to go out and beat the ice that had accumulated during the night off the ship. If the ship were to become top-heavy due to the ice build-up, it would tip over and sink.

It was King Crab season and we were watching over the crab fleet like a shepherd watches his sheep. The harsh weather was taking its toll on the fleet. They also had to beat the ice off their boats, and that took time away from catching crabs. Since crab season that year only lasted about four weeks, time was money. One of the boats, the "Crab Getter" (I don't remember the boat's actual name) had been neglecting the ice build-up on its mast and superstructure and had become top heavy. No one realized there was a problem until it was too late.

We received a Mayday call when another vessel realized the "Crab Getter" had vanished. We were only about twenty miles away, but the twenty-foot seas and driving winds reduced our maximum speed. We launched our helicopter (quite a trick in such bad weather) to look for survivors because it would take us about fifty minutes to traverse those twenty miles by ship. I knew that the odds of those men on the "Crab Getter" surviving were slim to nonexistent, so I began to intercede for their lives. A human can only survive for about five minutes in freezing water, so these men needed God to intervene if they were going to make it.

Almost as soon as I started praying, I felt like God was already answering—and the answer was "no."

I was stunned. I couldn't believe what I had just heard. Why wouldn't God want to save these men? Why wouldn't He want to receive the glory for such a miraculous intervention? I didn't understand. I argued with God; I pleaded with Him. But the answer was clearly no. After a few minutes I felt like God was letting me know that all the men were dead.

I wept for the widows who did not yet know that their husbands were not coming home. I wept for the children who no longer had daddies. I wept for the families that were no longer complete. I sensed that God also wept, but I still didn't understand.

When we got on-scene, we found the "Crab Getter" had completely overturned. All that was visible was the bottom of its hull. We searched the debris for bodies and found only one. Of the five-man crew, only one would go home to be buried. I stood outside in the driving snow and watched the "Crab Getter" sink beneath the waves. For a sailor, nothing is more depressing than watching a doomed vessel sink.

I had questions—lots of questions. Why did God say no? Why does God not explain Himself when He says no? Is it because I don't need to know the answer? Is it because He is God and I am not, and He doesn't have to explain anything to me? Is it because His reasons and purposes are part of a plan that I cannot comprehend?

Sometimes I really don't think I want the answers. We've all had well-meaning Christians pat us on the back and give us answers that don't help. I know they mean well, but I'd rather not have their help. If you've ever lost a loved one, or someone close to you, you know what I mean.

Did you know that God answered one of Jesus' prayers by saying no? In the garden of Gethsemane, with the cross looming over Him, Jesus asked if the cup could be taken away from Him. He even asked twice! He knew that God's answer was no, so He submitted to the will of God. Submitting to the will of God is not always easy for me; in fact, sometimes it is downright difficult. Knowing that Jesus could go on after His prayer was answered with a no, gives me some comfort. My salvation is a result of God's saying no and Jesus submitting to the will of God and going to the cross.

Ultimately I know that God is completely in control. Why did God allow those five men on the "Crab Getter" to die? I don't know. I won't have an answer until I get to heaven. At that time it will all make sense. Does that make it any easier? No. I simply choose to lean into the arms of my heavenly Father and trust His decisions and judgments. Since I know that God is in control, I must allow Him to be in control of my life. I may not like it when He says no to me, but I must trust Him.

I have only been able to come up with one answer for what to do when God says no. It comes in understanding this: Everything God does, He does to make us more dependent upon Him. When God says no, pray that He will use the situation to bring you closer to Him. This answer may or may not work for you. I pray that it does, but if it doesn't, I hope you're one step closer to an answer that satisfies. God always reserves the right to say no to our prayers. What we do with that answer will either draw us closer to God, or push us away. May we always use the "no" answers to pull us closer to God.

3
Finding God's Way Along the Military Path

Even with the military directing your steps, there can still be moments of wondering "What am I doing here? Am I making a difference? Lord, what do You want?" We've adopted something of a life-phrase for the God Allows U-Turns ministry. You'll see it in our offices, on our stationary, and on our signage: *The Choices We Make Change the Story of Our Life*. Even though God ultimately directs our paths, we have been given free will to make choices. Whether God takes us via a roundabout route or plops us down right where we know we should be, there's an indescribable peace in discovering God's plan for our lives. Even when we choose unwisely, He can still direct us back to the path He has for us and guide us through the storms until we are where He planned all along.

❧❧❧

I have learned to be content whatever the circumstances. I know what it is to be in need, and I know what it is to have plenty. I have learned the secret of being content in any and every situation, whether well fed or hungry, whether living in plenty or in want. I can do everything through him who gives me strength.

Philippians 4:11-13

∽: *Simultaneous Answers* :∼

SANDRA MCGARRITY, CHESAPEAKE, VIRGINIA

Before they call I will answer; while they are still speaking
I will hear (Isaiah 65:24).

At the closing of the church service, embarrassing, uncontrollable tears rolled down my cheeks. The Air Force was taking my husband away from me. This was the last service we would share for a while. We had been married for only six short months. He was going to Korat, Thailand, halfway around the world, for no less than six months. It could be dangerous. All of the troops hadn't been brought out of Vietnam yet. It was very near a war-torn area. Could life get any worse?

The next day we said our goodbyes and began the process of adjusting to a new lifestyle. I worked each day, went home, wrote letters, and went to church on Sundays. He worked each day, went back to the barracks, wrote letters, and eventually began to attend services at a Christian Missionary Alliance (CMA) mission for servicemen.

We each attended services faithfully, developed friendships, and did a lot of good works, yet something wasn't quite right. Since we both went to church and were pretty good people, we couldn't explain the restlessness, yet we both knew we were still looking for something.

About four months into the deployment, a church friend and military wife offered to loan me a book she'd just finished reading. It was a book about the return of Jesus, and that scared me. I didn't want to read about that. We never talked much about "the rapture" in church when I was growing up. I politely turned down her offer.

"Well, it's a great book and well worth reading," she answered. "Let me know if you change your mind."

About a week later, I was visiting another friend. This young woman's husband was stationed in Thailand with my husband. She did not attend my church and had never met the other friend. And yet, when I got ready to leave, she took a book from her bookcase and asked "Have you read this yet? If not, it's a book you should read. You can borrow my copy."

I saw the title. My heart sank. My defenses welled up, and I replied, "I really don't want to read that book. Another friend of mine tried to get me to read it just last week. I'm not interested."

"Why don't you want to read it?" she persisted.

"It's scary. I don't like those types of books."

She didn't quite laugh out loud, but she chuckled. "It isn't so scary. It's a good story about things that really are going to happen one day."

I tried to back away from the book. "I don't know about that stuff."

"Just take the book. If you decide not to read it, you can bring it back to me anytime."

"Okay." I sighed deeply as I took the book, somehow feeling this was not a coincidence.

I went home and got ready for bed. As soon as I was settled in, I picked up the book, just to glance at the first few pages. I put the book down when I had finished the last page at seven o'clock the next morning, just in time to get ready for work. I had not slept at all during the night.

I was miserable. On the drive to work and all throughout the day I prayed, "Oh, God, don't let things happen to me like what happened to the people in that book. I will do better. I will be good—I promise."

The remainder of the week went the same way—very little sleep—promises to be good—no peace. At the end of the Sunday-morning service, I went to the altar to pray the same prayer again.

In the middle of "Please, I'll be good," God spoke to my heart these words: "If you have to be good, why did I have to die on the cross?"

My pleadings stopped. I was awestruck. Why, indeed, did I think I had to do something to get what He had already done for me? There were no words said aloud, but I accepted what Christ willingly gave to me...and for the first time I fully believed it in my heart. That crushing weight and misery went away, and something came in its place. I didn't understand it, but it was good, and it was God. This is what it meant to be born again.

I was so happy that afternoon. I couldn't wait to write my husband to tell him about it. Then the thought struck. He has to have this too. He has to know this happiness. He has to ask Jesus to really live inside his heart. He has to understand this—if he doesn't we are going to have a rough time together.

I then prayed my first prayer as a new Christian, "Please, God, let him know You too. Let him have what I have."

I poured my heart out in a letter and put it in the mail that very day. At about the same time, my husband was writing to me as well—our letters crossed in the mail. A week or so later I received his letter. I won't quote it, but it read something like this:

> I've asked the Lord into my heart, and the change is unbelievable. You have to do this too, so you can understand what I'm talking about. I really hope and pray you will think about it because it's the greatest thing that has ever happened to me and because our lives are going to have problems if we don't feel the same way.

I was filled with joy because he also knew Christ as his Savior. I rejoiced because I knew by now he had received my letter. Both of our prayers had been answered; we had at last found that "something more." This realization of the power of God overwhelmed me.

My husband's letter told of his salvation experience. The meetings he had attended and the Christian men he was associating with caused him to take a deeper look at his own standing with God. After a Sunday night service at the CMA mission, an Air Force colonel had spoken to him about his relationship with Christ. Their discussion ended in the colonel showing him from the Bible how to trust Christ as his Savior. My husband had been excited at finding that "missing something," and his thoughts had turned to me just as mine had turned to him.

We had a couple of months to grow in the Lord before we saw each other again. There was quite a revival among the Air Force men during that deployment. Many men came to Christ. Many of those men are now in full-time ministry. Their homecoming was delayed for two weeks beyond the original date. I cried at the news but couldn't deny it was for the best. Many more men came to Christ during those two weeks of extended time in Thailand.

When my husband finally came home and we had time for long talks, we discovered another amazing fact. We had trusted Christ as Savior on the same day. Myself in the morning service in Myrtle Beach, South Carolina. He was at an evening service in Korat, Thailand. Because of the twelve-hour time difference, we had accepted Christ at very nearly the same time on the same day. God is so good—so good.

I don't know how our lives would have turned out if he had not been in the military at that time. I don't know what instruments the Lord would have used to turn us around. I do know that I am thankful for the military wives and the military men He used in our lives. I'm thankful for friends who wanted to share a book with me that encouraged me to take my faith deeper. I'm thankful that an Air Force colonel took the time to help provide for the greatest need he knew his men had—knowing Christ as their own.

And I'm thankful for a loving God who always answers the prayers of our hearts.

∿ *Basic Training* ∿

GLORIA PENWELL, CHATTANOOGA, TENNESSEE,
AS TOLD TO JENNIFER DEVLIN

WORLD WAR II WAS ALREADY RAGING in Europe, and many people felt it was right around the corner for the United States. People were beginning to enlist all over the country, and patriotism was rampant. Our family knew so many people in the military, it seemed inevitable my dad would eventually go and listen to the sales pitch of the recruiters in our town. Dad thought he would have only two options: enlist or be drafted. Being the eighth son of eleven children, he knew the importance of responsibility, and he knew how to depend on and support others. Many of his brothers were talking about entering the service as well, and they helped each other make the best decisions about where and how to serve. After meeting with the Marine recruiter, Dad found himself intrigued by the offer presented to him. In 1941, my father, Theodore Roosevelt Murray, became a Marine. Semper Fi!

After the initial paperwork and the official swearing in, the new recruit went off to basic training in San Diego, California. This was a world away to a young Michigan boy, but he loved the excitement of it all. Back home, in a little town called Bailey, his life had been simple and steeped in a rich Christian heritage. This new military life would give him reason to reflect on those simple times and thank God for the foundation of faith that was laid. Basic training was rigorous, but Dad continuously prayed God would get him through it, and that he would succeed in his new profession.

At the end of each training day, the men were exhausted. Many times, my dear dad would pray while lying in his bunk or while doing his daily activities. "Lord, I'm so ready to graduate from here. Where will I go next? What do You have for me, God? Lord, please keep me safe, and send me wherever You need me. My life is in Your hands." Day after day, he depended on God to get him through this new life so far from home.

The day finally came when the training was almost over, and assignments were being given out. There wasn't always

Theodore Roosevelt Murray. Semper Fi!

an official notice on a piece of paper. Many times the assignments were called out and bartered for like an auction house bidding over someone else's household goods. Who wanted to go here? Who wants to go there? Who will take this offer? That is exactly the situation my dad suddenly found himself in the middle of, late one evening in the barracks.

Everyone jumped out of their bunks the moment the commanding officer barreled into the room. They were all standing at attention, waiting to hear what critical news he might have for them. All the Marines thought it was strange when the officer began his bargaining,

"Who wants to go to Hawaii?" he called out.

Was this a joke? Everyone on the face of the earth would want to go there! Who wouldn't want to go to such a tropical paradise?

Well, my father began silently praying earnestly as they all stood there at attention. "Lord, give me direction…Lord, only if it is Your will.…Lord, please protect me from harm, and help me to decide whether to volunteer. Lord protect me from an impulsive decision." A constant stream of prayer flowed through his brain as the people around him clamored for the new beachfront positions.

The men all around Theodore shouted and placed their bids, causing quite a commotion in the room. My dad stood silently by his bunk, waiting for the chaos to subside. Eventually, the officer came up to dad's bunk and said, "You don't want to go, do you, Murray?"

"I'll do whatever you command me to do!" Dad replied.

"You don't want to go, right?"

"You're the commander, Sir!"

"Not this time," was the officer's final response, looking him in the eye with a stern and final tone.

Dad had been given an answer to prayer. He wouldn't be going to the tropical paradise, but he didn't care, as long as this was what God had for his life.

After the men graduated from basic training, those who volunteered for Hawaii were sent off to their new destination. They were excited and couldn't wait to enjoy the balmy weather and warm sandy beaches. But as we know from the history books, Hawaii experienced a tragic moment in December 1941, during the attack on Pearl Harbor. All of the men who volunteered that late night in my dad's room were present during the attack and were killed.

God's answer to Theodore Roosevelt Murray's prayer became more than guidance in a career; it was the merciful sparing of this young Marine's life. He realized through that series of events that God had something important planned for him.

"Lord, You spared me, and my life is Yours completely. Thank You for Your mercy and Your guidance. Show me what Your purpose for my life is"…came the humble prayer of the young Marine.

In 1943, while he was still in the service, my dad married a wonderful woman named Wanda. Their new life together had begun. Just a few years later, in 1945, Dad was medically discharged from the Marines.

He knew there was something more God was calling him to do. It was then he decided to go to seminary. He became a preacher, telling others of the wonderful God who spared his life. He preached in the pulpit for many years, until God began to shift his ministry focus. Theodore knew there were more people who needed the message God had laid on his heart. In the 1960s, he and Mom sold everything they owned and went to Mexico to start a home for orphaned children. They served there for more than forty years, bringing many children and adults to a saving knowledge of Jesus Christ.

God answered a young man's prayer in basic training one night. Then He took that young man, who knew the power of answered prayer, and answered the prayers of countless people across North and Central America through his preaching and leading.

God truly answers our prayers, and He can use anyone to impact lives for Him, if he or she accepts the role. I feel so blessed to have a father who prayed and then listened to the calling of Christ.

❧ ❧ ❧

❧ Rising Starr—Underwater Prayer ❧

HEATHER RUPPERT, NOKOMIS, ILLINOIS

I F I FELT ANY BETTER, IT WOULD BE ILLEGAL." That's what Frank Starr would say when asked how he was doing. Frank was *always* up, even when Alzheimer's was slowly stealing away his mind.

"He's a tough old bird," Eileen, his devoted wife, would say when she talked about him.

He must have been. He was part of the World War II generation. When his country called upon him, he served with his same signature enthusiasm.

Every veteran brings back a story. Whether he tells it, is up to him.

I am grateful Frank shared his story with us.

Seaman Second Class Frank Starr was a member of the crew of the U.S.S LST 946. On March 14, 1945, the Navy ship was performing practice maneuvers in rough seas off Bugho Point, Leyte, in the Philippine Islands. High winds and waves buffeted an amphibian tank, pushing it against the stern cable of the LST 946 until it became fouled and floundered in the water. The driver of the tank, an Army man, was thrown into the sea. Dazed and confused, he tried to keep his head above water by grabbing the anchor cable. His life jacket was only partially inflated. The merciless sea beat at him until it tore him off the cable, and he was left helpless in the waves.

"I'm going in after him," Seaman Frank Starr said.

"No, you're not!" his commanding officer ordered.

"Forgive me, Sir; I'm going in anyway, Sir!" Frank shot back as respectfully as possible.

"Do you think you can make it, Starr?" his commanding officer yelled above the roiling winds.

"I believe I can, Sir!" And Frank jumped in before anyone could stop him. He reached the other man and grasped hold of him, but the water was so violent and the waves so tall both men were pulled beneath the surface. Sensing they were sinking deeper, Starr knew he was powerless by himself to bring them back up. Frank and his comrade were cut off from air, but not from hope. In the dark turbulence he uttered a desperate prayer to God.

"I just can't make it without You, Lord! Help!"

And this is where Frank would pause in his story. I knew he was reliving it, as though it happened only days ago. Late in life, as he would retell this, his Alzheimer's would cause him to leave out parts. But I knew the story and could fill in what was missing. I knew it well enough that when he came to the part where he choked back his emotion, whether the right words came or not, I knew he was living it again. And I experienced it with him with a catch in my own chest, knowing I was in the presence of a man touched by God.

Hardly was the prayer completed before the answer came. Frank felt a powerful force, which he likened to a torpedo, propel him and his comrade back up. Their heads broke the surface of the water, and they were able to suck sweet air back into their lungs. With some effort, they reached the safety of a small boat.

The Navy didn't know whether to court martial Seaman Starr for disobeying a direct order or give him a medal for bravery.

The Army awarded him a medal of honor for risking his life to save one of their own.

When he showed off his medal, there was never personal ego involved. Frank never failed to give credit to God.

Frank Starr went on to be with the Lord on Monday, February 4, 2002. His body was buried at Camp Butler National Cemetery, Springfield, Illinois. His soul is now eternally safe and fully delivered into the hands of the One who rescued him from the sea half a century ago on the other side of the world.

His story of how God answered his prayer will live on forever as we share it with generation after generation.

❧ ❦ ❧

↵ *For God and Country* ↶

MAJOR JERZY RZASOWSKI, AKA "FATHER GEORGE," REDSTONE ARSENAL, ALABAMA,
AS TOLD TO JENNIFER DEVLIN

I HAD ALWAYS WANTED TO BE in the military. Growing up in Poland, I was part of the anticommunist movement, and I was very interested in seeing my country come out from under such oppression. I wanted my country to be a place of freedom—not captivity. During my teen years, I was intent on becoming a soldier, and my constant prayer was, "God, please let me be a soldier...please, I want to be a military man...if it is Your will, please let it happen."

I'll never forget the day I went to talk with the recruiter. I was so excited. I wanted to be a soldier, and this was going to be the first day of the career I longed for—or so I thought. The recruiter told me all about the great things I would experience and the places where I might be able to travel. He told me of future jobs that I had a chance of working toward. He went through so many details. At the end of his sales pitch, I asked him what I thought was a basic question. "Can I practice my faith in the military?"

With a smirk on his face, the recruiter replied, "There is no room for God in this military. Besides, who wants to waste their time with God these days? We are beyond that now." His smugness told me he had no idea what my faith in God meant to me.

"Well, Sir, then I cannot serve in this army," I replied. "I have to be where I can serve God too." I knew this was the end of my dream to be in the military in Poland.

Still, I continued to pray hard. "Lord, show me the way You would have me to go....You have closed this door, but please open another one....Show me what You want me to do and how I can serve You somehow."

Major Jerzy Rzasowski,
aka "Father George"

Later that year, I decided to enter a seminary where I could serve God all of the time. I knew God would answer my prayers and give me a wonderful life if I focused on Him. The seminary was a great place, and I enjoyed being there so much. Over time, I felt God calling me to do missionary work in Central America. "But Lord, how will I get there?" I prayed.

The diocese in Poland where I was serving had no money to medically treat missionaries who might get sick while in the tropics, so there was no way they would send me. They couldn't take the risk of having me come back to Poland with some disease, so they decided it would be best that I not go. Again I was stuck in a place where God seemed to close a door I so dearly wanted opened. But I kept my faith and moved forward in areas where God placed me.

Finally the opportunity came for me to go to Central America—by way of the United States. The plan was to send me to New York state, to a Buffalo diocese, from where I would be transferred to Central America after a few years. This way my health care would be covered.

Coming to the United States was amazing. Things were so different. Freedom dripped from the air. Buffalo, New York, was a new place, and God was about to do a new thing in my life. I was ready for whatever He had for me. God had placed me in a country that enjoyed the freedoms I so desperately wanted Poland to experience. I could finally see what living in a free country felt like. It was wonderful.

If this plan fell into place, I was really going to be a missionary in Central America! Exciting, but it wasn't going to be easy. I needed American citizenship and three more years in the diocese. So when the military recruiter invited me to join the U.S. Army for three years as a priest, I decided to accept his offer.

This time, instead of questioning whether I could practice my faith, the recruiter's response was not only "Yes," but "Yes, and we'd like you to be a chaplain." My prayer from years ago had been answered in the most unusual way and the most unexpected time. My heart cried out in praise to God for what He was doing in my life. I was finally serving God in the military. Central America would just have to wait…or so I thought.

Right after getting into the Army, I was told that I would have to go to Guantanamo Bay, Cuba, for a period of time. The shock on my face was hard to hide. At long last my prayers had been answered—I was a soldier, working in the Central American region of the world, and I was serving God.

I continue to thank God for the opportunities He gives me as I serve Him and my new country. It might have taken time and an indirect route, but God answered every prayer impressed on my heart…and then some.

❦ ❦ ❦

ᴧ *Flight for Freedom* ᴧ

Oscar T. Cassity, Major, United States Air Force, Retired,
as told to Gloria Cassity Stargel

Barely twenty years old in 1945, I was a new Air Force pilot serving in Europe. Orders came for me to fly into Yugoslavia—behind enemy lines—and rescue a group of twenty-six displaced persons of several nationalities, including some Americans. They had been hiding for months—in basements, in barns, and in the woods. They were now in the custody of a few friendly German officers who somehow had contacted our security, requesting help.

Orders further stated there would be no airport available. And, of course, it was necessary that I fly in undetected or get shot down. For those reasons, I was to take the absolutely smallest plane that would do the job.

The day of the mission, I reached the target area and landed on the designated tiny plot of pasture only to be greeted by—not twenty-six refugees—but forty desperate souls—all ages, few speaking English.

A quick prayer went up, "Lord, what to do?" I simply did not have space for forty. Yet they faced almost certain death from starvation and untreated health problems or from the Nazi forces, should they be discovered. I couldn't bear to leave even one behind. God answered my prayer within a split second when I became convicted of my only option.

I told a couple of our crew: "Estimate the weight of each person and add them up. We'll factor in the weight of our remaining fuel and determine if our aircraft can get off the ground if we take them all."

The fact that the refugees were undernourished—and therefore very thin—was to their advantage right then.

We pushed the limit, deciding to take them all. I had them sitting in the aisle, three abreast, with orders, "Do not move. Do not shift your weight."

Finally loaded, we rolled down the short, grassy makeshift airstrip, straining mightily to gain the optimum 100 knots for take off. "Forty knots, Sir," my co-pilot called out. "Fifty knots."

"Sixty knots." Trees at the end of the runway loomed dead ahead. At 80 knots, I dropped the quarter flap and forced the plane up, my landing gear brushing the tops of the trees.

When we reached 6000 feet, I went back to tell our passengers, "We're out!"

A sea of faces smiled broadly.

Tears rolled down cheeks.

Prayers of gratitude went up.

But not one person moved—not an inch.

During the following years in my military career, I experienced many hair-raising missions—combat flights in Europe and Korea, tight flights for the Berlin Airlift, unique flights to the South Pole—missions that required prayer and received help from God. Yet that memorable moment aboard the little packed plane remains one of the most satisfying. I can still see those forty expressions—expressions that proclaimed louder than words the absolute joy—of freedom.

✎ *Bitter, Beaten, and Made Better* ✎

MARK GERECHT, COMMAND SERGEANTS MAJOR, HUNTSVILLE, ALABAMA

> Trust in the LORD with all your heart and lean not on your
> own understanding; in all your ways acknowledge him,
> and he will make your paths straight (Proverbs 3:5-6).

IN JUNE 2002, ALL MY DREAMS SEEMED to come true. I was a Battalion Command Sergeants Major stationed in Korea, with a wonderful wife of twenty-one years and a great daughter who was just two years old. What more could I ask for? It seemed my life could not get any better. Little did I realize my life was about to spin totally out of control.

Perhaps the two darkest years of my life were about to begin. I was surrounded by immoral conduct, leaders who were motivated by political gain, and, perhaps most disheartening of all, I was not making the best decisions to resolve the problems and challenges at hand…no matter how hard I tried. I began to rely on my experience and understanding rather than placing my faith and trust in Christ.

I was working fifteen to eighteen hours each day, six and seven days a week. No matter how hard I tried, things kept getting worse. I began to become bitter and felt beaten and worthless. But there was a bright spot…we had recently found out my wife was pregnant with our second child…something we both wanted badly and were joyfully looking forward to.

Then in May 2003, while away on temporary duty, I received a call from a neighbor. My wife was in a Korean Hospital and needed to undergo emergency surgery. I arrived at my wife's side around three in the morning. The doctor informed us we had already lost our unborn child and that my wife needed to undergo surgery immediately. We had difficulty understanding what was going on and our options due to the language barrier. Eventually we were able to convey to the doctor that we still wished to have children. He assured us everything would be all right, and the surgery would take about two hours.

I prayed hard during her surgery for the Lord to protect my wife. I asked Him to give the doctor wisdom and expertise. True to his word, about two hours later an orderly came to get me. I thought he was taking me to the recovery room; instead, he took me to the operating room. After they put me in scrubs, I met the doctor.

"You have a difficult decision to make," he told me. "I cannot save all of your wife's reproductive organs. If you choose to keep them, she will have to undergo chemotherapy. If you choose to remove them, she will not be able to have children again."

Looking at my wife unconscious on the table, I felt helpless and alone. My wife and I had not discussed this option prior to her being put under anesthesia. I swallowed hard and told the doctor to take the damaged organs—I couldn't take the chance of losing my wife. I reasoned we had one healthy child and things would somehow be okay.

I made arrangements for my mother-in-law to be with my wife during her recovery because I felt compelled to be with my unit. Within two weeks, while my unit was in the field undergoing its annual certification, I received notification that my father had had a heart attack.

Receiving the news of my father's heart attack was yet another devastating blow. With twenty-two years in the Army and thirteen of those spent overseas, I was torn between loyalty to my unit and being with my father. I chose to return home to be with my father.

My return to duty shortly afterward was met with severe admonishment from members of my command. They felt I should not have left in the first place. This drove me deeper into bitterness and, for the first time in my twenty-two years of service, I felt as if I had failed in some way. I became increasingly angry with the members of my chain of command. They seemed to be motivated by other factors and appeared to have no concern that we had just lost a child and I had almost lost my father.

It was then God sent a friend to our home in Korea. As we spoke, he called me on the carpet about my bitterness and anger. He also admonished me that I needed to let go of these things and pray for the individuals who were treating me wrong. He said *I* had to change if I wanted my *circumstances* to change. In my heart I knew he was right, but I found this very difficult to do. Forgiveness can sometimes be a very bitter pill to swallow, but eventually I did as he suggested. I prayed God would help me to forgive them, help me to do what was right, and perhaps most importantly, guide me according to His desires and not mine.

Things began to drastically change after that. I was suddenly transferred out of Korea, back to the United States, and into an assignment I came to enjoy very much. My commander and his assistant are perhaps the best leaders I have ever worked with in my military career. It was like going from night to day.

Within a month of my return to the States, my father underwent two additional surgeries. I was grateful I could be close to him during this time. As a result of God's plan and His grace, we were also provided the opportunity to build a house that could accommodate my parents and our family, creating the ideal environment for our daughter to get to know and enjoy her grandparents.

I believe God sent my friend to speak to me and to help me realize I needed to get rid of my bitterness and anger. He taught me to trust in the Lord with all my heart and not to depend on my own understanding, but to seek His will in all I do. My worries have been dramatically reduced, but, more importantly, I find life is much easier when I allow God to be in control. He provides inner peace and replaces bitterness with love. Had it not been for the helpful intervention of my friend, I don't believe I would have been delivered from this situation in a positive way.

My family is stronger, my daughter spends time with her grand-parents, I am learning another side of leadership from excellent role models, and I have learned much from my past mistakes and poor decisions. God showed me mercy, grace, and love during a dark time in my life.

Now I utilize every chance I have to help others as I was helped. I am far from perfect, but now I know and understand that God can change our lives—but we may have to change first.

4
When God Says to Pray

IT'S LATE AT NIGHT. You're just dozing off to sleep when your loved one stationed overseas is suddenly in your thoughts. You smile, think of him or her lovingly, and try to get to sleep, but sleep won't come. Or maybe you're standing in the grocery line and you have a deep and urgent bad feeling for your son, husband, father, mother, daughter, sister, or brother stationed in harm's way. They're thousands of miles away, so what can you do? When all else fails, we pray. But did you ever consider…maybe God put that special someone on your heart at that moment because he or she needed you right then? God urged you to prayer because He had a way out and wanted to use your prayers to accomplish His will. Amazing! He knows us so well.

⋘⋙

*Do not be like them, for your Father knows
what you need before you ask him.*

MATTHEW 6:8

∾ All the Fullness of Heaven ∾

CARON GUILLO, AMARILLO, TEXAS

I T WAS ONE WEEK AFTER Saddam Hussein's army invaded Kuwait, and I had just been given the message to bring my husband's pistol and sleeping bag to the airfield.

I piled the kids into the car and raced to Biggs Army Airfield, home of the Army's air defense artillery. I found the gate I needed and asked the guard for my husband. Soon Bob appeared, and I handed him the requested items through the opening. He nodded to the left, so I followed him along the fence, Nicole on my hip, Christopher's small hand in mine, until we stood several feet from the guard. Through the chain link barrier, Bob and I exchanged brief kisses.

He knelt down to press his lips to the cheeks of his children. "I love you, Buddy," he said to three-year-old Christopher. "You help your mom."

He smiled at baby Nicole. "Bye, Princess. Daddy loves you."

I refused to cry.

"Come back at nine tonight," he whispered to me. "I'll be allowed outside the gate for a few minutes." He glanced down at the children. "Come alone."

I understood. It would be too difficult for him to say goodbye to his children a second time.

I'd begun praying earlier in the week, when Bob first hinted that he might be deployed. He had been right. He was scheduled to leave the next morning, August 12, 1990, leading a handpicked group of soldiers on the first flight out of Fort Bliss. Ten thousand men eventually followed.

But that afternoon I continued to pray while gathering more things Bob might need. We had no idea the plane would be so loaded down with equipment that the men could take only what they carried on their backs. They chose weapons and ammo over sleeping bags and personal items.

At nine o'clock that night, I went to the airfield for a final goodbye. Other women showed up—wives of the non-coms under Bob's command. We stood in the parking lot just outside the gate, trembling like middle-school girls waiting for their first dates to arrive. One woman brought huge commissary bottles of shampoo and tubes of toothpaste.

"I'm not going to summer camp," her husband laughed.

Another brought a roasting pan filled with beef and potatoes. She didn't want her husband to be deployed hungry, so she handed a fork to him, and he stood by their truck eating out of the pot.

Bob and I chuckled at those men and women, our friends. Then we hugged and prayed and hugged again. The men headed back to the hangar from which they'd emerged. The gate locked shut behind them.

I drove home, checked on the children, and climbed into a lonely bed. Before shutting off the light, I phoned Bob's parents and mine, asking for prayers. Then I did something inconceivable even to me— I slept peacefully.

That night I'd fallen off the emotional cliff on which I'd been teetering all week. To my surprise, God's comfort and love provided a safety net to break my fall. I would cling to it desperately in the months to follow.

A few days later, I watched the evening news to see Saddam promise to send thousands of Americans home in their coffins if the two countries should clash. Fear leaped into my heart, and tears spilled down my cheeks. In a prayer of wavering faith, I was soothed and reminded that Perfect Love—God, Himself—casts out fear.

I wrote in my journal that night: "The Lord of all holds all things in His hands. If God does not bring Bob home to me, He will take him home with Him. What more could I ask than that?"

Weeks passed. I tried to keep busy. Christopher and I often prayed together for his daddy, and our young son confidently made plans for his father's return. Phone calls were rare. E-mail was non-existent. One October day was especially difficult as the loneliness of our home chased my thoughts to Bob. That afternoon I wrote in my journal: "This bittersweet time has drawn my heart and Bob's closer, encouraged our trust and faith in the Lord, and turned many souls to our God. Isn't that the paradox of Christianity? Hearts wounded to the point of breaking, yet filled with all the fullness of heaven. How precious it is to be precious to God—and how secure is His strength if we claim it."

Christopher, normally as pragmatic as any three-year-old, amazed me with his certainty that God would bring Bob home safely. I, on the other hand, fought fear and dread every hour as January brought the promise of war. But I also kept going to the Father for the comfort and strength only He could provide.

In February, Christopher woke up excited. It was his fourth birthday. "What time will Daddy call?" he asked expectantly.

My heart sank. Bob had been somewhere along the Iraqi border since November, and the Gulf War had been going on for a month. Even though I'd prayed for a birthday call, I knew the facts, so I told Christopher, "Sweetheart, Daddy's a long way from a telephone."

"That doesn't matter," our son replied. In Christopher's mind, the circumstances weren't an obstacle for his heavenly Father.

Not long after, the phone rang, and Christopher gave me an I-told-you-so smile.

"It's your grandparents," I said on my way to answer it. No one responded to my hello for a moment.

"Hi, Honey." The voice sounded tinny.

My heart thumped. "Bob?"

"Yeah, how are you?"

I knew to slow down when we talked. Otherwise the long dis-tance delay over a military phone would cause our words to be lost on top of each other. Never-theless, I rushed ahead. "How'd you manage to call?"

He chuckled. "You're not going to believe this, but a gen-eral showed up at our camp today. It was my job to give him a tour. Afterward, he asked how long it'd been since I talked to my family. When I told him it had been weeks, he had his driver take me two hours to a phone."

I spun around to where Christopher sat eating his toast and smiling. "You mean you didn't plan this call?"

"I wanted to, but there was no way."

"In February, Christopher woke up ex-cited. It was his fourth birthday. 'What time will Daddy call?' he asked expec-tantly." Above, father and son reunion.

I smiled back at our four-year-old. "Someone was expecting to hear from you."

As my two guys talked, I contemplated how part of God's plan for us is simply to learn the joy of belonging to Him.

Two weeks later, Bob participated in the invasion that officially ended the war. Few Americans were killed—the predictions had been thousands *per day*—and I felt incredibly humbled. How often we forget to whom we pray. "A defeat of almost biblical proportions," I read in some news magazine. Exactly.

On March 27, 1991, Bob's unit arrived home at Biggs Airfield at four-thirty in the morning. I figured I'd break down in tears when I finally saw him. Instead, God gave me laughter.

Though my heart resisted the whole experience, I thank my Father for what He taught me. One of the greatest lessons came from Christopher. I cried out to the Lord in prayer and depended on His power, but my son prayed with complete confidence. Blind faith, some might call it. Childlike faith, Jesus said.

Christopher never once doubted that God had everything under control. Our little boy saw the outcome of the faith he already possessed. I believed in God, but Christopher *believed God.*

I want to grow up to be just like that.

᪥ *My Brother, My Only Brother* ᪥

PAMELA JOHNSON, BUCKLEY, WASHINGTON

MY STOMACH KNOTTED AND I CRIED every time a plane flew over my house. My usually quiet neighborhood lay below a military flight path to a nearby base. Aircraft swarmed to Fort Lewis like bees to a hive. The jets' roars served as a constant reminder: My brother was in a naval vessel just miles from the Iraqi shore, and he was in harm's way. The television news anchor confirmed my worst fears. Our country's soldiers were in combat—Operation Desert Storm had begun.

A few days later I had dinner with a woman whose brother was stationed in the Persian Gulf—just like my brother. At the time we didn't know what the outcome of the war would be, but it felt refreshing to know that another sister loved and worried about her sibling as much as I did mine. I asked her if people ever tried to dismiss her feelings by saying something like, "Why are you worried so much—he's only your brother?"

"Oh, I get that a lot," she said, "but I just tell them, 'He may only be my brother, but he is my only brother.'"

Her words offered encouragement. I didn't realize how much strength they gave me until the next day when one insensitive woman told me it was nice I cared, but there was no way I could care as much as a mother or father—it just wasn't the same. Another woman tried to reassure me by saying, "Well, at least you're not next of kin."

In one respect I agreed with the first woman. My love is different than my parents'. But there is something about a sibling's love that is special. Siblings are the people you can count on when life gets rough and you need to spare Mom and Dad's emotions. As a sister of a naval man during the Gulf War, I was the one who heard about "the mine the ship almost hit" and "the incoming missile that ran out of gas." Those aren't the kinds of things my brother chose to write my parents about, but dear old sis heard the uncensored version.

As a sister during the Gulf War, I had a lot of other responsibilities on the home front too. Besides reassuring a little brother of his family's love even though he was miles away from home and facing a war, I also tried to cheer my parents up when the situation sounded grim—like when the bombing campaign was televised or when several media people announced that the liberation of Kuwait had begun.

I still remember the night the war began. Dad told me his only prayer was to have Toad (my brother's nickname) home alive and in one piece. I knew he also had another concern—Toad's homecoming. Dad didn't want my brother to suffer the lack of welcome he had received when he'd returned from Vietnam.

"Dad," I said with all the courage I could muster, "I'm praying and I have faith Toad's coming home, and he is going to come home a hero. I promise."

I did everything I could to support my brother. I baked cookies. I went to every military rally I could, even though I'm shy and reserved. I held prayer meetings for the soldiers in my home. I sold yellow ribbons. I wore yellow ribbons. I tied ribbons around my mailbox, schoolchildren's arms, and my car's antenna. I encouraged every child I met or who visited my home to draw a picture for a soldier, and I guaranteed the postage to the Persian Gulf.

When I had a break, I remembered our childhood. Like the time Toad and I got in a tiff and wrestled for over an hour, and our parents came home just in time to rescue us from each other. How we fished on our great-grandfather's pond and shared s'mores around the campfire. I envisioned a long-haired teenager leaving for boot camp and coming home an enlisted man with a military haircut. The entire family teased Toad about his stubby head—I called him my buzz brother.

On some nights I wondered if Toad would ever get to hold my daughter—the niece he had never seen. I questioned whether the hug I received before he boarded the plane bound for his ship's homeport would be my last from him. It had been two years since that hug, and I hadn't seen Toad since. Sometimes I wished I had squeezed him a little bit longer.

After sifting through my memories of Toad, I felt sorry for the thoughtless woman who said I wasn't "next of kin." Perhaps she never had a brother like mine or like the ones of the many local siblings I met during the Middle East crisis.

One sister insisted that a nearby town's city council hang flags up in honor of the troops. Another from my local area hauled a sign as big as a barn door to a military rally with her brother's name sprawled across it. And a man from my hometown quietly ached for his little sister every time he saw media pictures of Iraqi soldiers.

The Gulf War had made me and many others reaffirm and strengthen our family ties. For this loving sister, the war not only united a country—it united a family. It built a great faith.

Toad came home shortly after the cease-fire of Operation Desert Storm. My family planned a big welcome home celebration. Plenty of relatives, neighbors, and friends eagerly waited at the airport. The group dressed in red, white, and blue. Each waved a small flag and several held signs.

Finally the jet arrived, but something was wrong—no one got off the plane. *Is Toad coming back?* I wondered. *Is my brother really on the plane?* I could tell my father had the same thoughts. His brow wrinkled. His tired eyes lowered.

Then over a loud speaker a ticket agent announced the reason for the delay: The pilots and passengers were giving the military personnel on board a standing ovation. All of the passengers would be unloading shortly.

I instantly felt relief. I turned to look at my father. His face glowed. He smiled. After months of sadness, the sparkle in his eyes had returned. His son had come home a hero.

Finally we could see Toad hastening down the corridor. He beamed. He would get to meet his niece for the first time, and I would get to hug him again after all.

I looked up.

"Thank You for answering my prayers," I whispered, "And thank You for my brother—my only brother."

~: The Eyes of the Lord :~

Kimlee Saul Worrell, Fayetteville, Georgia

The events of 9/11 are indelibly etched in the minds of all military families; they changed our lives, our mission, and our culture forever. But when I reflect on the events of that day, my mind reflexively goes back four days prior, which is when the intercession actually began.

On September 7, 2001, I found myself completely overwhelmed by a burden to pray for an Army chaplain who had been stationed with my husband several times throughout his career and was presently stationed in Korea. "Pray Psalm 91, pray Psalm 91" ran through my mind incessantly throughout the day. This burden created tremendous concern, since Psalm 91 is a psalm of protection. Military wives frequently pray this psalm over their spouses during deployments. After praying this psalm throughout the day, I finally sat down in the late afternoon and zipped a quick e-mail off to Seoul.

Sent: Friday, September 7, 2001 6:54 PM

Subject: Psalm 91

Am praying this psalm over you today…for a hedge of protection all about you. May you be bold and fearless in your obedient service, confident of that assurance. K.

In my own mind, I was really asking, "If the Lord has me praying Psalm 91 over you, what is going on?" I checked our in-box several times over the next few days, but there was no response. There was also no respite from the prodding in my spirit to continue to pray for our friend.

Even on 9/11, the burden didn't lift. Despite the tremendous prayer needs produced by the tragedy, the Lord still had my attention arrested on the possible needs of one Army chaplain in the Korean peninsula. I read through Psalm 91 many times each day and intentionally spoke those verses aloud as requests before the Father. The next day I sent yet another e-mail:

Sent: Wednesday, September 12, 2001 4:33 PM

Subject: just a follow-up

Still Psalm 91—God bless—K.

There was still no response. I continued to press on in prayer for another seventy-two hours. On the third day, I received an e-mail from his wife, who had remained stateside during his tour in Korea:

> Sent: Saturday, September 15, 2001 5:56 PM
>
> Subject: Pentagon attack
>
> Bob was in the Pentagon when the plane hit and was involved in the aftermath. The attached is his journal narrative of those events. As you read it, please pray for him. Especially pray for the many others involved at both the Pentagon and in New York.

I read the attached journal entries and wept all the way through the reading. I wept in grief over the events described and in wonder at the incredible specificity of God's Word. Evidently our friend had been on temporary duty at the Pentagon when the attack occurred. His journal described his location in relation to the site of impact and his exit through smoke-filled passages.

The Lord had led me to pray for four days preceding:

> You will not fear the terror of night,
> Nor the arrow that flies by day,
> Nor the pestilence that stalks in the darkness,
> Nor the plague that destroys at midday.
> A thousand may fall at your side,
> Ten thousand at your right hand,
> But it will not come near you.
> (Psalm 91:5-7)

My friend chronicled how the chaplains in the Pentagon at the time had immediately set up ministry tents outside the building. He described how they went back into the building time and again to bless the dead and help evacuate and minister to the wounded.

The Lord had led me to pray:

> If you make the Most High your dwelling—
> Even the LORD, who is my refuge—
> Then no harm will befall you,
> No disaster will come near your tent.
> (Psalm 91:9-10)

He took note of a terrible stabbing pain in his foot and leg and marveled at the fact there was no apparent injury.

The Lord had led me to pray:

> For he will command his angels concerning you
> To guard you in all your ways,
> They will lift you up in their hands,
> So that you will not strike your foot against a stone.
> (Psalm 91:11-12)

Reading through that narrative, I felt like crying out like Daniel: "There is a God in heaven who reveals mysteries" (Daniel 2:28)! It impressed on me in a "forever way" the need to be obedient to those intercessory burdens the Lord lays on our hearts. Those mysterious moments when He gives us a specific scripture to pray over a specific person at a specific time over a situation that is entirely unknown to us! For truly, the need to pray had been inexplicable to me. I thought this chaplain was in Korea, but a Sovereign Lord proved true to His Word: "The eyes of the LORD range throughout the earth to strengthen those whose hearts are fully committed to him" (2 Chronicles 16:9).

He had His eye on His servant, and He called the body of Christ to prayer. How I praise Him, and how I thank Him for convicting me of the need to pray. May we all learn to listen to His still small voice.

⚛ ⚛ ⚛

∽ *"I Thank God You Come Home Safe"* ∾

PAT KNOX, ST. LOUIS, MISSOURI

MOM, MY UNIT IS BEING ACTIVATED, and I'll be leaving for Iraq in two months." These are words a parent never wants to hear. How do you show your support for your child and at the same time calm your own fears? How do you release your only son, the one who will carry on the family name? The son who is so young and stands at the door of an uncertain future?

I have always been an unwavering supporter of the war against terrorism and the war effort in Iraq. I am proud and humbled to be an American and proud that we are a people who are willing to stand and even fight for the freedoms that we believe in.

But I'd never been asked to sacrifice my only son. Would my commitment remain firm when my son was in harm's way? So many questions flooded my mind as I pondered the possibilities and the reality of being separated by time and distance from the boy I loved. These questions and fears are inevitably common to all parents, spouses, children, relatives, and friends as we face an uncertain separation; however, I also believe God is there to meet each of us uniquely, to walk with us and to calm our fears.

For me it began a few years earlier as I watched my teenage son push beyond the boundaries he had been taught. I struggled to determine what I could do to make him choose the path I desired for him. I lay awake nights, unable to sleep, and replayed every concern while searching my mind for new methods of approach. After exhausting my abilities and affecting my health, I was brought to a state of surrender. I was ready to admit I could do nothing by myself, but I could do "everything through him who gives me strength" (Philippians 4:13).

I was powerless to bring about change in anyone else, even my own son. I could only allow God to change *me*. My inadequate abilities were transformed through reliance on God's unlimited resources, and my anxious mind was replaced with God's peace. God was gracious to remind me He loved my son more than I. That truth comforted me, and I released him and his future to God, determined to just love him and pray for him. I didn't know God was preparing me, even then, for a greater challenge to come.

Those two months passed quickly, and there were times that the questions and "what ifs" would begin to surface. Each time, as God reminded me of His love, His presence and peace would return. One such reminder came the day of deployment. As there were some last minute things to do, a trip to the bank to sign "power of attorney" papers resulted in a divine appointment...a "chance" encounter with a local, popular professional football player. Upon learning of my son's imminent departure for Iraq, he asked if he could pray with us. His anointed prayer brought us into the presence of God.

As I left the bank, I headed to work, where I am a producer of a local Christian radio talk program. When I was asked to come on the air and discuss my son's departure, I remember saying, "I know there is a very real possibility I will not see him again this side of heaven. If that happens, I can truly say I am at peace with it. I know where he will spend eternity since I had the privilege of being the one who led him to trust in Jesus as his Savior." I talked for some time and never came close to tears, which in itself was a miracle. Anyone in my family would tell you that even a TV commercial can bring me to tears. But God had indeed prepared me, and the peace I felt was beyond understanding.

What I didn't know was my husband had been listening to the broadcast, and he called me immediately. He is usually the strong one, but he had been moved to tears by the strength he heard in my words. The strength and the peace were real, and God supplied it for me the entire time my son was in Iraq.

An unexpected blessing came through the radio station and my church. I had the opportunity to develop a friendship with an Iraqi family who had immigrated to America only a few years earlier. The husband had been in Saddam Hussein's army during Desert Storm and, by God's design, I was visiting in their home the very day my son was flying to Iraq. This family encouraged me with their prayers and kept me informed of many positive changes in their country. Their appreciation of the sacrifices that many American families were making to give their country and their families a future was tangible evidence of God's provision.

When my son returned home, I eagerly planned to introduce him to the Iraqi family that had shared so many prayers and so much of their heritage with me. We set a date for them to join us for dinner. The day came and once again God served up another divine appointment. By "chance," we met on the weekend of the historic first free election in Iraq. We rejoiced with them as they jubilantly displayed their proof of voting, the "purple index finger." But the most memorable and treasured moment of the day, the "crème de la crème," was when the Iraqi wife entered my home and headed straight for my son. In her broken English she said, "You soldier? Thank you for my country. I pray for you every day. I thank God you come home safe."

∻ A God Thing ∾

JANET LYNN MITCHELL, ORANGE, CALIFORNIA

I KNEW FROM EXPERIENCE the weight that one carries when they have a loved one serving in Iraq. A heaviness had reminded me to pray—almost hourly, for my brother-in-law. But Rusty had come home, and he was safe. Why had the heaviness returned today?

I had returned home from taking my son, Joel, to school when I felt the urge to pray for the daughter of a woman I knew, who was serving in Iraq: "Lord Jesus, I ask that You protect Jennifer Sphar. I ask You to give her strength and wisdom as she serves our country in this struggle." I finished my prayer and began to tidy the house. Yet within minutes, I found myself in prayer again, asking God to protect Jennifer. By noon, I couldn't count the times I had stopped to pray.

Standing by my sink, I made up my mind. Even though I knew Leslie, Jennifer's mom, was at work, and even though I had only called her twice in ten years, I picked up the phone and called her house. When the answering machine picked up, I left a message that I had been praying for Jennifer that day.

Later, while I was preparing dinner, my mother called and said, "Janet, have you heard? Leslie and Steven Sphar are on the news. Just hours ago, their twenty-year-old daughter Jennifer was hit by a mortar shell. She's alive, but injured." Stunned, I explained to my mom how I'd been praying for Jennifer all morning and had even called Leslie earlier in the day.

Now I understood. The heaviness I felt was a good thing—a God thing, as it brought me to my knees in prayer. That morning I only knew I needed to pray; God knew Jennifer was in the line of fire.

Listening to that still small voice of God when we are convicted to pray is a spiritual discipline I have grown to better understand the older I get. Yet no matter how many years pass, I am always in awe at how He works in our lives.

Corporal Jennifer Sphar is currently stationed at Camp Pendleton. Her unit is soon scheduled to redeploy for their third tour to Iraq. On April 27, 2004, Corporal Sphar received a Purple Heart for the injuries she received that fateful day—the day I fell to my knees and prayed.

ᴗ: *Cool Breezes* :ᴗ

Jean Adams, Fort Knox, Kentucky

It was hot that year at Fort Polk, Louisiana, and I mean steamy. It was 102 degrees in the shade, with almost as much humidity. The kind of hot that when you step outside, you're instantly damp and wonder why you bothered to dry off after your shower. It was during this sweltering heat wave that the cavalry was practicing in the field. My scout husband, Staff Sergeant Tom Adams, was part of that fine group of men and women of the 2nd Cavalry Regiment, a light readiness training regiment of the Army. They were in the middle of the Kisatche National Forest doing some basic recon training. I, being a military wife of about twelve years at the time, knew they would be in full gear during this exercise. Full gear consists of their battle dress uniform, a Kevlar helmet, a weapon, load-bearing equipment, and boots. I was hot just thinking about it.

Staff Sergeant Tom Adams—recipient of cool breezes.

Suddenly I felt led to pray for them, especially for my husband. I had been taught to be specific with God, so I asked for Tom, my husband, to be blessed with some cool breezes. Knowing that God was fully capable to do exceedingly above and beyond what we can think or imagine, I prayed, "In the middle of this heat wave, God, send Tom cool breezes from heaven." I then went on about the busy business of being a mom to three young children.

A few days later when the field exercise was over and Tom was home relaxing, he said, "I've got to tell you about the neatest thing that happened out there."

Knowing this could be any number of possibilities with an Army scout for a husband, I said, "Tell me, Honey, what was it?"

"Well, we were all sitting down waiting for one of the guys on patrol to show up. I was sweating buckets when all of a sudden a cool breeze refreshed me. I asked the others if they could feel it, but they couldn't. They all thought I was crazy, but, Honey, I felt it. I know I did."

I had such a great time telling him God had answered my specific prayer. It encouraged us both, showing us nothing is impossible for God. I knew heavenly breezes had cooled him off. Praise God. He certainly does answer prayers.

❧ ❦ ❧

∽ *One Lifetime and Five Miles Apart* ∾

Eva Marie Everson, Casselberry, Florida

My father's words shook me to the core. I fell to my knees.

"Baby," he said, "it's multiple myeloma."

Years previous, for a decade and a half, I'd worked in the medical profession. I knew about multiple myeloma. What it meant.

It was a death sentence.

"It's not like it used to be," Daddy interjected, as though he'd read my thoughts. "The doctor at the Medical College of Georgia says he doesn't believe in 'no hope.' He says we can beat this thing."

This was too hard a thing to hear—me a whole state away and not able to hold him. When I could find my voice, I reaffirmed Daddy's faith—both in his doctor and in our God. Six months later, I sat in my father's living room, laptop poised on my thighs as I attempted to meet a deadline, while my father snoozed comfortably in the nearby recliner. In a few days, he would have a final procedure—stem cell replacement—and then, by God's mercy, we could bring this chapter of our lives to an end.

My father snorted, then jerked, opening his eyes. "Did I fall asleep again?"

I returned the smile. "You did. But you need your rest."

Daddy removed his glasses and ran his fingertips over closed lids. "You know, I was just thinking about Jack Taylor. Do you know who I'm talking about?"

In spite of Daddy being the consummate storyteller, I hadn't heard of Jack until I was in my forties—the day my brother and I cleaned out our mother's attic and found boxes of Daddy's military memorabilia. Tucked inside a leather wallet (made in Libya, Africa, and intricately etched in desert colors), was a small black-and-white photograph of two young men, arms draped over each other's shoulders. Comrades in wartime. "That's Jack Taylor," my brother said. "You know, Daddy's Air Force buddy."

I surmised this was a subject fathers and sons discussed. I couldn't ever remember hearing the name. Now here I was, hearing it again.

"Your old Air Force buddy?"

"Yeah," he said, replacing the glasses. "Jack M. Taylor from Gastonia, North Carolina." He chuckled. "Funny how I can remember that, and I can hardly remember yesterday."

I nodded.

"I wonder whatever happened to him."

I looked over at the screen of my laptop, powered up to the Internet. My nimble fingers typed in the name of a search engine. "Jack M. Taylor?" I said.

"Jack M. Taylor," Daddy repeated. "We went into the Air Force the same day. September 6, 1949. Both of us alone when we went in—him from North Carolina and me from Georgia. No friends going in with us, you know. We met up in New Orleans. Him, me, and Joe A. Sims. The three of us all alone. Traveled to Lackland together and went through basic."

I pulled up "people search." "Gastonia, North Carolina?" I asked.

"711 North Ida Street," he said. "I don't think the street even exists anymore."

Nevertheless, I typed in the address, marveling that the cancer treatment had not affected Daddy's memory one bit.

"Daddy," I said a moment later. "There's a Jack Taylor in Gastonia, North Carolina."

He looked at me in wonder. "How do you know?" he asked.

"I just pulled it up on the Internet."

His smiled warmed my heart. "Is that right?"

"I can give you the number, if you'd like. You can call him."

It was the wrong Jack Taylor.

Daddy hung up the phone. I could sense the sadness. How do you lose a person you were so close to for so long? *Father, help me find him. For my daddy...*

"Tell me more," I said.

"Jack and I were both assigned to the Supply Division in basic. After thirteen weeks we went home for a month, then met back up in Denver. When we were done there, we both signed up for ETO. Do you know what ETO is?"

I shook my head, keeping my eyes on his face, but my fingers on the computer's keyboard. Somehow I would find this man, I determined. *Please God. Let him be alive.*

Daddy chuckled again. "ETO is Eastern Theatre of Operations. We thought we'd go to Italy or England or France. We didn't know we could end up in Africa, but we sure did." Daddy shifted a bit. "In May 1950, we went to Fort Dix, New Jersey, where we waited for our assignments. We had some good times there."

"You did?" I asked, my eyes now on the computer screen. There were several Jack Taylors in North Carolina. I wondered which one, if any, were *the* Jack Taylor.

"One afternoon they called for volunteers to go up to New York and be a part of a live TV audience. *The Ted Mack Original Amateur Hour.*"

"You were on TV?" I asked, my eyes wide. The things you learn...

"We sure were." He quieted for a moment. "Then one night we shipped out. We went first to Grand Central Station, then on to Overfield, Massachusetts. A few days later we boarded a C-54 aircraft. Went to Newfoundland and then to the Azor Islands. We were flying at 30,000 feet to Morocco when the word went through that the Korean War had begun."

I pictured him sitting in that plane. Him and Jack and Joe Sims, who I'd not begun to look for.

"We landed in Morocco, then took off for Tripoli, Libya, where we were stationed for the next eighteen months."

"Daddy," I interrupted. "I've found more Jack Taylors."

"Let me have the numbers," he said. For a while, he tried to find his old pal, but to no avail.

"Tell me more," I finally said.

"We were in Africa on the hottest day ever recorded: 137 degrees in the shade." Daddy laughed. "And there ain't no shade. I worked in the supply office. Jack worked in the warehouse, so we didn't see each other during the day. But we'd eat our meals together and, of course, we were housed together. On weekends we'd take off and do stuff."

"What was it about Jack that made you such good friends?"

"All three of us, really," Daddy said. "Jack and Joe and me. It was just something about our characters. All coming from small towns. None of us partyers. We didn't get drunk or gamble." He laughed again. "Shoot, we only made $76 a month, so there wasn't much to gamble with." He rested his chin in the palm of his hand, his elbow on the armrest of the chair. "It was a camaraderie you only find in the service. Anyway, after a year and a half, I figured we'd be out by Christmas. Maybe New Year's. Then, on December 1, I was sitting at my desk working when Jack came to the door. 'You aren't going home?' he asked me.

"What do you mean?" I asked.

"'They were supposed to let you know hours ago. We're going home. You'd better hurry,' he said.

"I did what they call 'clearing the base.' I bought a small piece of luggage, threw everything I had in it, and ran for the plane, barely making it. After eighteen months, the three of us were going home. Thirty days later we met up in Great Falls, Montana, where it was forty below zero. Can you believe that?"

I said I couldn't. I also couldn't believe that I couldn't find any more Jack Taylors. I focused on Joe Sims, from Mississippi.

"September 1952, we were supposed to get out—we were in West Palm Beach by then—but they extended our stay. In November Joe left to enroll in college, and then I left when my brother was killed in a car accident. Jack surprised us all. He reenlisted and was sent to Guam." Daddy's blue eyes darkened. "Jack came by the Georgia State Patrol station where I was working in 1955—I don't know if I was married to your mama by then or not—and I've tried several times to find him since, but…"

"I'm sorry, Daddy," I said. "I can't find any evidence of Joe Sims either."

Daddy nodded, then his brow shot up. "Jack had a sister with an unusual last name. Look this up," he said, spelling it. "Look it up in North Carolina."

Bingo! We'd hit the "Jack"-pot.

Later that evening, Daddy made *the* call it'd taken forty-seven years to make. "Do you know who this is?" he asked. There was a pause. "Go all the way back to 1952, and you might remember," he said. Then he laughed. "Yeah, it's me, Jack. It's Preston."

Jack had made a career out of the Air Force. Married, had two sons. And where did he live? Five miles from my home.

Thank You, Father!

Daddy survived cancer and will visit my home this summer, when he and Jack will reunite. They talk on the phone often, sharing old memories and making new ones.

They continue in their search for Joe.

5

A Greater Sacrifice

THERE IS NO WAY TO EXPLAIN the fear a military family goes through when a loved one is in combat. Any knock on the door, even if expected, puts a stone in your belly and a lump in your throat. Opening to find dress blues (or dress whites or class A's—it doesn't matter) standing on your doorstep rips both your breath and heart out while turning your knees to rubber. Nothing will ever prepare you for it. And nothing can prepare the wounded soldier for a life without limbs or basic abilities. But there is One who will keep the sacrifice from being in vain. One who loves and comforts and understands beyond our power to express. Our Father understands sacrifice. He knows our hearts and our pain. And He will see us through in His perfect love.

❧❧❧

Greater love has no one than this, that he lay down his life
for his friends . . . this is my command: love each other.

JOHN 15:13,17

ᴠ: *Man on Fire* :ᴠ

Bʀɪᴀɴ ᴀɴᴅ Rᴏɴɪᴇ Kᴇɴᴅɪɢ, Bᴇᴅғᴏʀᴅ, Tᴇxᴀs

Tʜᴇ ᴀɪʀ ᴡᴀs ᴄᴏʟᴅ ᴀɴᴅ sᴛᴇʀɪʟᴇ, just like any other hospital. It was the middle of the night and the stabbing pain in my left leg yanked me out of a fitful sleep, beckoning for yet another round of pain medication. The ward was quiet except for the sound of paced breathing. Before reaching for the nurse call button, I looked across the room to see my roommate with his arms extended, rapidly rotating them so that his straightened fingers traced small circles in the air. He whispered cadence to himself, "One, two, three, four," and continued his motions until he was exhausted and his arms fell to his side.

I was an eighteen-year-old Army basic trainee at Fort Benning when I injured my knee in a training accident. Less than forty-eight hours later, as I recovered from reconstructive surgery, I asked God if He had sought me out to ruin my life, or if He just didn't care. You see, I had wanted to be a solider from as early as I could remember. My father was a Vietnam vet and a career Army officer, and his father was a World War II Army vet. As far back as you can trace the family tree, men of my family have served this great country—it was in my blood. I was so anxious to become a soldier, I pre-enlisted just as I was beginning my senior year in high school. There was nothing in life I wanted more than to be a soldier, but an injury of this magnitude crushed those hopes.

Despite being in the Deep South, Georgia gets very cold in February. I shared a room with Lieutenant Rico, who had severe frostbite on his hands. He was a young lieutenant attending the Mountain phase of Ranger School at Fort Benning. While on a long road march, he spent the night exposed to the cold night air. His concern for the troops in his charge was so great, he forgot about himself. One of the dangers soldiers face in cold weather is not direct exposure, but the greater susceptibility of sweaty hands and feet to frostbite than dry skin. For this reason, troops rotate their socks and glove liners at regular intervals with a spare dry pair. Distracted and in a hurry, Lt. Rico did not change his glove liners and the frostbite began its damage unnoticed. By the time he realized his mistake, he was in danger of losing his hands.

Admittedly, my medical prognosis was not as devastating as having to face life without my hands. In surgery, the doctors and surgeons had to work quickly on my knee because the injury was worse than they predicted. The procedure took longer than they expected, and I had lost too much blood for them to continue at their regular pace. Once the anesthesia cleared, the doctors gave me the news. The surgery was, for the most part, a success. However, I would forever walk with a limp, never run or play sports again, and would suffer from premature arthritis. The 110 staples required to close the thirteen-inch incision were not encouraging. The exciting dreams I had for my future were now like a blank movie screen—still, silent, lacking any sign of life.

Recovering in a semi-private room, I was an unintended participant in the doctor's discussions with Lt. Rico. His diagnosis was harsh—he would lose one hand for sure and most likely would lose most of the other. I thought, *Well, at least I can commiserate with someone else whose life has been wrecked early on.* I thank God that Lt. Rico didn't see it that way.

Neither of us slept much during those first few days so we talked a lot. A combination of pain, medications, eighteen hours a day in traction machinery, and nonstop hospital traffic made sleep nearly impossible. It's amazing how well you can get to know someone when you share extraordinary circumstances, confined to a ten-by-twenty room. Whenever my roommate wasn't spinning circles with his arms extended, he was reading his Bible, or writing letters as best he could with his Mickey Mouse-looking bandaged hands.

I was angry and hurt, warmed by the flicker of my self-pity and toying with deep bitterness. The rest of my life would be miserable. But Lt. Rico was telling me that God has a plan for each of us, sometimes in opposition to our own desires. He encouraged me to look beyond today and past the bed that had become a prison. He shared with me how having a vision fuels passion for something beyond us. "With God," he told me, "all things are possible, and we must choose to follow Him if we want to see the impossible take place."

The doctor's conversations with Lt. Rico were dismal, but he never had the same sense of doom I felt. With utter conviction he told everyone, "There is no way I am going to my wedding without both of my hands." He lived what he talked and took on his prescribed physical therapy with fervor. If the physicians told him to soak his hands for at least two minutes at a time, he pushed through the horrible pain and immersed them for five. If physical therapists said do fifty extended arm rotations every three hours, he completed one hundred every hour. His conviction, determination, and passion told me this was a man on fire, the embodiment of the ideal soldier.

Every dawn brought with it new excitement. The doctors made their rounds shortly after sunrise. The first few days, doctors arrived expecting to have the amputation surgery later that same day, but when they removed the bandages his hands had incredible improvement. Each day more people crammed into our little hospital room—doctors, nurses, technicians, and even administrators had come to see Lt. Rico's miracle. About ten days after admittance, he walked out of the hospital with fully restored and functional hands, except for the last inch of one pinky.

Lt. Rico was a leader and a true Ranger. He did not leave me, a spiritually "fallen" comrade, behind. His example opened my heart and inspired me to follow his lead. I quit asking, "Why, God?" The circumstances were no longer important. Now I wanted to know, "What's next, God?" Praying for strength and healing, I gave everything to recuperating. The next six months were the sweetest misery of my young life. If the therapists said do ten leg curls with ten pounds of weight, I did twenty curls with twenty pounds. When they said ride the bike for twenty minutes with ten percent resistance, I rode for thirty minutes with twenty percent resistance. I sweated and cried buckets. I became a man on fire.

Fifteen years later, I can still hear Lt. Rico huffing and puffing, doing his circular therapy exercises at oh-dark-thirty, and I'm still inspired, especially when the cares of this life start to tug me down. My scars are a visible, but joyful reminder of what I learned and how far I have come. If you ask me about them, I will tell you the story with a smile on my face.

You see, God took what I originally thought was a hopeless situation and introduced me to my wife and laid the foundation for the rest of my life. Today I enjoy intramural sports. I walk and run without a limp and without pain. I wrestle and play hard with my four beautiful children (and sometimes even with my beautiful wife). I have received a blessed healing only God can give. Looking back, I'm glad it didn't turn out any other way.

I have lost touch with Lt. Rico over the years, but I do know that because of the power of prayer, and his unrelenting faith, he walked down the aisle with both of his hands intact, just like he said he would. And I bet, if you ask him about what happened to his little finger, he would tell you the story with a smile on his face.

✌ No Leftover Courage ✍

GLORIA CASSITY STARGEL, GAINSVILLE, GEORGIA

THE CALL CAME IN THE MIDDLE of a scorching Saturday afternoon. Our younger son, Rick, stationed at Cherry Point Marine Corps Air Station in North Carolina, had been admitted to the hospital with a ruptured appendix.

Fear took over as I suspected the worse. A ruptured appendix can prove fatal. "We'll be there as soon as we can," I said, but we were two states away.

"Oh, God, please help Rick," I quickly prayed.

I called my husband, Joe, in from mowing the lawn and, frantic, he phoned Camp Lejeune, locating the surgeon. "Yes, I operated on your son this morning," the surgeon said. "The infection had spread into the surrounding tissues. We're leaving the incision open in case we have to go back in."

My courage vanished. That means peritonitis had set in.

"Lord, please help," I continued to pray.

"I have to tell you," the doctor added, "he's a very sick boy. But he's young, and he's in good physical shape. I think he'll be able to make it."

Joe and I began the long drive to North Carolina.

Joe never talks while driving, so I had practically all night to think—and worry.

Why in the world did Rick wait so long before seeing a doctor? Then my wandering mind reasoned: Why am I surprised? The Marine Corps obviously teaches its men they can withstand anything—that they're invincible.

I should know. Joe himself is a Marine to the core. *Semper Fidelis*—always faithful. He enlisted at age seventeen and now, with the rank of major, served with a reserve unit in Atlanta. The fact that Rick followed in his dad's footsteps shouldn't have surprised me.

Continuing my reverie, I contemplated the crucial factor that had influenced Rick—and affected us all for that matter. Four years earlier we had faced another surgical crisis, when Joe was diagnosed with incurable cancer. Although he appeared to be beating the odds, the outcome was uncertain. It had been particularly demoralizing for him when the Marine Corps declared him medically unfit to serve. Just recently, though, he had been reinstated to active status and even dared to hope for a promotion in rank.

This specter of uncertainty about his dad's health clouded the years Rick was in college. The week he received his degree, he had his hair cut short, shaved off his beard, and joined the Corps. "Somebody's got to carry on the tradition," he explained.

At three o'clock in the morning, we reached Camp Lejeune's hospital. Inside our footsteps echoed down dismal hallways. A squeaky elevator emptied us onto the third floor where at the far end a small lamp revealed a desk and the silhouette of a nurse bent over her paperwork. We approached her and asked about our son. She looked up, gave us the once-over, and said, ever so kindly, "Would you like to see him?"

"Oh, yes! May we?"

"Follow me," she said. With that, she picked up a flashlight, flicked it on, and cut us a path down the black asphalt-tiled floor of yet another gloomy corridor.

"He's in the room with another patient," the nurse said softly, motioning us through a door. "We'll need to be as quiet as possible."

We could barely detect Rick's bed in the shadows. Following the sounds of muted groans, being careful of the IV-dispensing contraption with its tubes and bottles, I touched his shoulder. His hospital gown was drenched with perspiration. "Rick," I whispered, bending close to his ear, "it's Mother and Dad."

A very groggy son answered, "I'm glad you're here."

I leaned over and kissed his fevered brow, "I love you."

"Love you, too," he managed, then drifted back into a medicine-induced sleep.

"Lord, our boy here needs Your healing touch," I prayed. "And, Lord, about that courage—I need it now, real bad."

Rick was alert the next day—Sunday—but still feverish and miserable with pain.

On Monday morning, Joe let me out at the front door to the hospital while he found a parking space. The hallways, quiet all weekend, bustled now with activity. White-uniformed nurses and corpsmen hurried in and out of rooms; patients—all wearing U.S. Navy-issued blue cotton robes and scuffs—did their prescribed walking.

When I reached Rick's room, he lay flat on his back, anxiously eyeing the door. "Where's Dad?" he asked hurriedly, a note of excitement in his voice.

"He's parking the car."

"Can you help me get up?" he said, painfully pushing the sheet back with his feet and with great effort raising himself on one elbow, "I've got to be standing when Dad gets here."

I sensed this was no time for questions. Taking his arms while he clenched his teeth against the pain, I pulled him around into a sitting position on the edge of the bed, and then sat down beside him. While he held his incision with one hand, he placed the other one around my shoulder. I, in turn, put one arm around his back with my other hand steadying us with his IV pole, and somehow we stood. We propped the back of his legs against the bed for support. Then he motioned me to ease away.

Just in time. Masculine footsteps in the hall. "Sh-h-h."

Joe barely got inside the room when he stopped in his tracks, not believing what he saw: Rick, standing by his bed. Whereupon Rick pulled himself to almost-full height, snapped to attention, and with a crisp salute heralded, "Congratulations, Colonel, Sir!"

"Wha—wha—what?" Joe stammered, totally bewildered.

"Your promotion came through," Rick reported, a big grin forming. "Colonel Asher called this morning from Atlanta. You're a Lieutenant Colonel."

"Promotion? Called *here?* How did he find me here?"

To describe Joe as dumbfounded would be a gross understatement. He was undone. Oh, but for a video camera to record the event! Suddenly it all sank in, and his face lit up like the Fourth of July.

And, just as suddenly, the Marine in him sprang back to life. With his officer demeanor engaged, he "snapped to," and—even though he was wearing civilian clothes that ruled out an official salute—returned Rick a quick, informal one. "Thank you, Lieutenant."

Then with two long strides Joe reached Rick and enfolded him in a giant bear hug. I joined in to make it a threesome. We laughed and cried, all at the same time, realizing that probably no promotion ever came at a more tender moment.

After we helped Rick back into bed, he furnished a perfect finish to the stirring scene. Reverting to his affectionate title for his dad, he said, "We're awfully proud of you, Pa."

Pa, the new Colonel. We were "just family" once again.

Yet, I dare say, a changed family. For etched forever in my heart is the picture of that young feverish Marine in a wrinkled, bob-tailed hospital gown, barely able to stand, snapping to attention and "promoting" his dad! What a memorable moment! What courage! Semper Fi—to the core!

I borrowed some of that courage the next day when Joe and I left for home. Our tear-mingled embraces followed three lump-throated goodbyes.

Yet as we drove away, I felt at peace, confident that our boy would get well. For the surgeon had pointed out Rick was young and strong physically. Now, with that memorable moment, God had allowed me to see evidence of Rick's inner strength as well. My faith was secure once again. God was looking after our son…and me.

But where was my faith, my courage, early on in this experience? I am reminded of something I once read: "There are no yesterday leftovers of courage."

For it is true—courage must be renewed daily.

And so must faith.

✌ *Beautiful* ✌

Jennifer Devlin, Huntsville, Alabama

It was springtime, a time of new growth and new beginnings. Churches were gearing up for the celebration of our resurrected Lord. Stores were full of springtime gifts and chocolates galore. It was not the time to watch someone enter heaven's gates—but this was God's timing, so there we were.

Full of hope, I traveled with a friend to the hospital to visit this beautiful lady, praying all the while. "God, may Your will be done in this. What is Your will in this? What should I be praying for exactly?" It was hard to watch her suffer, and we knew that God could perform a miracle, but was that His plan for her right now? We parked in the hospital lot and entered with arms full of cheerful gifts to remind her of a time without sickness, even though our minds were full of heavy thoughts. All we heard walking down that hallway was the clicking of our shoes against the cold hospital tile.

We loved her so. A sister in Christ a fellow friend from our Bible studies and congregation. This was a lady who had brightened so many lives. She had embraced many new military families when they moved to town and had shown them the love of true friendship. Their family was forever faithful to the military chapel, serving behind the scenes in more ways than anyone will ever realize, impacting our military community in immeasurable ways.

Her homeland was a nation and an ocean away, but that did not stop her from helping friends everywhere she went. Her native tongue never got in the way of her love for others. She was an instrumental part of our Korean ministry in the church, leading and encouraging other Korean women who had married American military men. She stood in the gap between the two women's groups in our church, building relationships and bridges, all in the name of Christ. A role model of true servanthood and true friendship—whether anyone took the time to notice or not.

She was married to the love of her life, a man who had swept her off her feet so many years ago…and continued to do so daily. They lived the storybook life of a couple who met because of military circumstances, but had made a lifetime commitment to each other as a result. She was his love from a far-off land. He was that handsome man in uniform she had met many years ago, and he had been a dedicated, loving husband. God had blessed them with the birth of a wonderful son, who was now grown and in the military himself.

So why was God about to take her? These are the thoughts that flooded our minds as we walked down the hall to the elevator. A woman who would pass away too early in life…it seemed so unfair, but we knew God had a higher purpose…and we knew that someday soon she would be with her heavenly Father. The pain would be over soon. No matter how our prayers were answered, we knew that God would be glorified somehow.

As we entered the room, there was such a sweet spirit there. No doom and gloom and hardly any sadness. Just a woman who clearly loved the Lord and rested in His presence. We could see the love of Christ all over her peacefully resting face. She was short on time, but long on faith. Because of her illness, her body was fading fast. She wasn't interested in taking medication; something in her countenance told us she was ready for what Christ had promised. She was ready for eternity. Breathing was labored and speaking was down to a whisper. All the strength she had went to opening her eyes and to the occasional phrase uttered from her lips.

We sat and held her hand and told her about whatever we could think of, and we could tell she was listening but also thinking about other things. She finally let us know that she wanted us to sing some songs. We were not choir members, or even women with great voices, but we complied with our dear sister's request. She wanted to sing, so we sang. We made a joyful noise. We sang praise songs to the Lord right there in the hospital room. Nurses came and went, leaving us to our time of worship with our friend.

We could tell that she kept up with each song, chiming in with her labored whisper when she had the strength. Yes, she loved the Lord. Yes, He had made her glad. Yes, she would rejoice (and even managed to clap her hands). What a sight! In the midst of such illness, here was a sweet angel who took every breath she had to praise her Lord and Savior—to rejoice in all circumstances. This will always be a visual reminder of the verses found in Philippians 4:12-13 that tell us to be content in every circumstance, and in the New King James, it reads, "I know how to be abased, and I know how to abound. Everywhere and in all things I have learned both to be full and to be hungry, both to abound and to suffer need. I can do all things through Christ who strengthens me." She embodied these verses.

Her husband and son came to visit too, bringing lunch and a smile for their beloved. They talked to her, joked a bit, and thanked us for the visit. When our dear sweet SolCha saw that her son was there, we were instantly in the midst of a desperate cry from mother to son. "James, do you believe in Jesus? Are you a Christian?"

Barely a whisper could come out, but the force of the tone made it clear she meant business. He chuckled a bit, and though uncomfortable with such a strong question, replied, "Yes, Mom, I'm a Christian."

"No joking…(a long pause)…you believe?" she whispered in a strong quiet yell.

"Of course, Mom," he assured her. There was a thick coat of seriousness in the air of that room but a sense that relief was felt in her heart at that moment.

We knew that our dear friend was making peace with her family, and she wanted to know for sure that her son would be with her one day in heaven. Now she knew. She was at peace. A few minutes later, when everyone else was busy talking, she grabbed my arm, and pulled me close.

"Heaven…" She could barely get the word out, but the smile and the glory on her face made me know she saw more than was in her room. Somehow I knew what she was trying to convey.

"Do you see it?" I asked.

"Yes…it's beautiful…" That was all she could get out, and then she was too worn out to talk more. She closed her eyes once again and lay there peacefully with a sweet smile and glow about her face. She was in the presence of the Lord. She was in a beautiful place in her mind.

We prayed with her and with her family. As we got ready to leave, we didn't know if we would see her again. I had no idea this would be the last image of her the Lord would place in my mind—the remembrance of a dear friend etched for a lifetime. She went to heaven shortly after Easter. Our prayer that God's will would be done was answered. She wouldn't have to suffer more in this body, and she was resting peacefully in the arms of her Savior. He had taken her home.

I have thought about her many times since then, and how much her last days have changed us all. The women have bonded in a stronger way through helping her family. Their son has a renewed dedication to faith and to the military. He has a stronger purpose— to serve with the same passion his father did and to find a wife with the same gentle loving spirit as his mother.

My mind always goes back to the joy I saw on her face. She had seen a glimpse of heaven…and wanted others to know the wonder of what she saw. What a vision she must have had! What hope that gives us all for the future. "Who shall separate us from the love of Christ? Shall tribulation, or distress, or persecution, or famine, or nakedness, or peril, or sword?" What a verse that is for us in Romans 8:35 (NKJV)! Even in the midst of death, illness, and the life after this one, we as Christians can cling to the knowledge and hope that there is a life afterward…and it must be glorious…beautiful even.

↳ The Walk ↵

DE'ON MILLER, LOVINGTON, NEW MEXICO

AFTER HE COULD WALK WELL on his own, my three-year-old son would invite his father for a walk. "We go to walk now, Daddy?"

I used to stand and watch them from our living room window. It would break my heart to watch them walk. I can't say exactly why it hurt so much. After all, they looked so beautiful, the two of them lost in a world of their own. The small left hand of a little boy, cupped and held up by the big right hand of the daddy. The younger walked on the outside, for his dad must have known that the path was much smoother for him there, though it appeared as if the younger led the elder. It was a slow walk, not very far, through clots of red dirt alongside the plowed field of a local farmer.

We lived in a small town in Texas. Several mobile homes surrounded our own. We were a small group of people, centered between a lonesome highway and a field of dirt—this field of dirt where Aaron would take his daddy to walk.

I never knew exactly what they talked about on these walks. It was their time, and I was never given a clue from either of them as to the words that flowed back and forth between father and son. Perhaps, for Aaron, it was like a sweet secret, and for Doug...well, Doug and I didn't talk much back then. When we spoke, it was usually to argue. Our marriage was ending, and it was a slow and painful demise.

For a while, each day was always the same. "We go to walk now, Daddy?"

"Come on, Little Man," his dad would say.

Off they'd go, and I'd stand at the window, looking and wishing. Now I can't even remember what my heart must have wished for.

Things changed, and we divorced. Now when Doug called, Aaron asked his dad, "We go to walk?" But during these times, his little voice quivered and then broke.

Doug and I both loved him so much. At one point Aaron went to live with his daddy for a while. Then, finally, it was back and forth. Perhaps he was too young to voice his feelings to me about all of this then, but I know he must have voiced them to someone else, for I've been granted the privilege of reading at least a part of these conversations, rendered in Aaron's own young hand.

I don't know when the prayers of my son were written. I found them several years ago. By his penmanship, it's evident Aaron was just learning to write in cursive. I remember all the practice hours he spent back then. Cursive writing covered our phone books and used pieces of mail. His wobbly words were everywhere. He must have

Lance Corporal Aaron Austin,
November 2003.

been in the third grade when he wrote the first three prayers.

Aaron would watch me read, then mark and write in this blue book, and at some point, he must have felt inclined to do the same. For on a particular page, there are the numbers from one to sixteen, with each number being circled. Circle number one: *Help me learn about God.* Circle number two: *Help dad with taxes.* Circle number three: *Help mom and dad stay to gather.*

The first three prayers are written in blue ink, circle number four is skipped and beside circle number five, written with a pink felt-tip are these words: *Help Roy and Doug be friends.* Circle number six is skipped and circle number seven is in the same pink ink: *June 15, Thur. 1993, help Greg and De'on be happy.* So, these last two prayers were written at a later date than the first three. Circle numbers eight through sixteen are empty, without written words. It became a confusing life of parents, stepparents, stepsiblings, and assorted family challenges.

He used to say, "I wish my whole family could all just live together in one big, happy house."

It must have been the twenty-eighth of April when Captain Teague called to tell me the time and place Doug and I could meet the arrival of the plane. It had to have been the date, because, despite all the noise in my home, with everyone's cell phone ringing at once, friends and relatives talking in every corner, delivery people bearing flowers too sweet, despite all this commotion and upset, I can still remember sitting there in my bathroom, and out of desperation, ripping off that page of the pink inspirational calendar that constantly had to be re-bent, re-folded—something, anything—to prop it back up on the back of the uninspirational toilet.

The date of this page is the twenty-eighth of April. That day I kept those words close to my heart. Today, these words rest in a small trunk, ornamented in brass and hand-painted in hues of antique white, stenciled with roses. That pink page I take out from time to time gently reminds me:

> Let us live in the blessing of Today...
> Cherishing our memories, but not holding them too tightly...
> Treasuring our dreams, but not building our future on them.
> Let us live in the present, rejoicing in the gifts
> God lends to every moment of Today.

I called Doug right after Captain Teague and I finished our phone conversation. Then, as I was seated there on the closed lid of the toilet, I gazed up at the white rose wrapped in a layer of waxed paper, its frail color barely faded, its perfume now only imagined. It stands at attention, pressed between two layers of glass. It is a rose separated from the rest of its family. One tiny part of my memories, those blessed memories of mother and son.

This much is all very clear to me.

I don't remember now what time the arrival of this important flight was to be, but the plane would land in Oklahoma City, several hours from my home. I remember feeling hurried. But mostly I remember Doug's words to me, "De'on, I just want to walk with him one more time."

I think my response must have sounded something like, "Okay, Doug, I'll be there. We'll have to get all our stuff together because we won't have time to come back here. We'll meet you in Amarillo."

It must have been something like that because we gathered our stuff, and Greg drove us to Amarillo. I sat and I listened to the chain beat against the flagpole and a bird sing. It was such an odd mixture of tones to me at the time, while we waited for Doug and his middle son to arrive. To meet us there at the funeral home, just off of I-40.

Dad. Mom. Eric. The three of us close together. For Aaron, we made the long drive.

Hours later, in Oklahoma City, it was hard to miss hearing the heavy dragging and pushing of such a burden, from rear to front, of wood over steel, over and over and over, as those Marines, just as strong as their load, escorted and lowered the crate that held the casket. The flag-draped casket of Lance Corporal Aaron Cole Austin, United States Marine Corps, Killed In Action on April 26, 2004, Fallujah, Iraq.

And the three of us walked those few steps with others. Not a long distance at all. In fact, it was only a short walk from the commercial cargo jet door to the door of the hearse. And we all walked together, together and beside this final armor. Our own.

We walked.

The local newspaper in Amarillo reported that over three hundred cars drove behind us in the long and slow drive that day. To lay him to rest, dressed in his Blues, ornamented in brass. I remember people standing out in the fields, fields of plowed dirt. Some of them surely must have been poor souls out there that day, without some temporary home. Perhaps they felt as lost as we did on that third of May. They spoke to us in a symbolic language: beating their chests with their fists, then holding their palms open and up, emulating our pain, touching their hearts as well as our own, saluting my son's final ride and those who followed. And we follow.

I remember our families turning into a family. And I think that surely Aaron must have been smiling up there with Jesus, knowing his prayers had finally been answered—but at what cost? Watching father and mother, stepfather and grandmother, brother, uncles, cousins, and aunties, all holding and helping and leaning. Gathering.

Now he is waiting for us in that big, happy house.

Yes, Roy and Doug are friends. As they hugged.

As we hugged.

As we walked.

As we talk even now. And all of us are "to gather."

As we heal.

∴ A Gift of Peace from Iraq ∾

PAMELA HALLAL, INDIANAPOLIS, INDIANA

ONE MAY THINK MY JOURNEY as a Marine mom began in May 2003. But the truth is the journey began the moment my obstetrician said, "It's a boy!"

Before my son, Private First Class Deryk Hallal, was breathing his own air, I made a commitment to God to raise him to know the Lord Jesus Christ. I prayed continuously for his salvation and for the life God would lead him to live. At the age of seven, he accepted Jesus Christ as his Savior. After two years of asking to be baptized, and feeling confident of his understanding of baptism, my husband and I agreed.

Deryk chose to quit college only nine weeks before graduating with a degree in computer programming. He said, "I am not going to waste one more day of my life doing something I don't want to do." I felt a devastating pain arise within my soul. He was so near completion of a several-year process. It was difficult for me to understand how he could so easily give it all up. It's very clear to me now how God had called him to fulfill a greater commission.

I was often asked how I could be so calm amid a time of war, knowing my son was in the U.S. Marine Corps. I answered confidently each time with this statement: "We, along with many others, are praying unceasingly for God to protect him spiritually, physically, and mentally." Philippians 4:6-7 (NKJV) says, "Be anxious for nothing, but in everything by prayer and supplication, with thanksgiving, let your requests be made known to God, and the peace of God, which surpasses all understanding, will guard your hearts and your minds

through Christ Jesus." I believe in the truth of God's Word that says "whenever two or three come together in His name, He is with them" (Matthew 18:20).

But in the early evening of the sixth of April 2004, while seated in the family room of our home, along with two Marines clothed in their Dress Blues, I strongly questioned God's Word. How could God choose to take my gorgeous, six-foot-five-inch, patriotic, joyful, beloved son from this world?

Internally I was struggling, insisting it had to be a mistake. The external events around me told me otherwise. Why hadn't God answered our prayers? What purpose could this possibly fulfill? Why were we now

Private First Class Deryk L. Hallel—"Of everything I learned in boot camp, this is the biggest thing: Praise God all the time, not just when you're in trouble! God will be there and has a plan for you, no matter what you think."

embarking on the most traumatic trial of our lives? My heart's desire was to see my son grow into a successful, courageous, God-honoring, and God-fearing young man, who would make the right choices in life with as little pain and tribulation as possible. I forgot God ordained his life before he was even born.

Several weeks later, on a spring day in May, I received an answer to many of my questions. The First Sergeant assigned as our casualty officer arrived at our home with a box of our son's personal belongings shipped in from the battlefield of Al Anbar Province, Iraq.

Not much was in that box. But laid among some clothing, loose change, and a pair of combat boots was a treasure we will cherish the rest of our lives. Written on twelve index cards was the personal testimony of our son, Private First Class Deryk L. Hallal.

Deryk had been invited to give his testimony to our youth group upon returning home after his seven-month deployment. He never had the opportunity to do that—at least not in person. Tears streamed down my cheeks as I read those twelve cards. I had been confident our son was with the Lord. At that moment, I became more assured than ever. On those twelve index cards are written the following words:

> Good morning! My name is Private First Class Hallal of the United States Marine Corps. Where you are sitting, I myself was sitting five years ago. Growing up, how many of you can remember when you missed church? I can practically count the times. My family was at church every Sunday and Wednesday unless my parents were sick or we were on vacation.
>
> I really didn't listen to God when I was in Youth Group or when I was in church. I kind of did what I wanted to do, and talked or didn't pay attention, which some of you most likely do now. I grew apart from God and knew I wasn't on the same page with God as I should've been.

Back in February I decided to join the military. I asked God to show me what He wanted me to do with the rest of my life. Well, the day before, the U.S. started war with Iraq. So after a couple of months working two jobs, it was time for me to go to the hardest and longest boot camp in the military.

"For I am the LORD, your God, who takes hold of your right hand and says to you, 'Do not fear; I will help you'" (Isaiah 41:13).

I got to boot camp on May 19, 2003. I had everything from the civilian world taken and put into a little box that would be stored for the next three months. But there was one thing no drill instructor could take from me. That is my faith.

My first day, I asked myself, "What did I get myself into?" Well God led me to the Marines. Every time I got I.T. [Incentive Training] I said, "God is my strength," and I thought of these verses in my head: "Be my rock of refuge, to which I can always go; give the command to save me, for you are my rock and my fortress" (Psalm 71:3); "for you have been my hope, O Sovereign LORD, my confidence since my youth" (Psalm 71:5).

Every night since I was nine years old, I prayed to God about the next day. In boot camp I prayed to God twice a night.

The Crucible of the Marine Corps was the hardest thing I have ever done. Now you might be asking me what the Crucible is. The Crucible is a test of mental and physical power. The Crucible is a two-day event where each night you get four hours of sleep. In those two days you hike fifty-six miles with a ten-mile hike on the last morning.

"Consider it pure joy, my brothers, whenever you face trials of many kinds, because you know that the testing of your faith develops perseverance. Perseverance must finish its work so that you may be mature and complete, not lacking anything" (James 1:2-4).

The Reaper is a hill that is ninety degrees and six hundred yards up. Imagine after seven miles of hiking that you climb the Reaper and still have four miles left until you're done.

Now imagine doing the whole Crucible of fifty-six miles with a blister the size of a baseball on the ball of your foot and trying to walk all fifty-six miles with some running, also.

After the Crucible, I had four layers of skin removed from my foot. I was in so much pain the last twelve miles that I squeezed the rosary in my hand so hard that it made a Jesus on the Cross imprint on my palm.

"He heals the brokenhearted and binds up their wounds" (Psalm 147:3). "And call upon me in the day of trouble; I will deliver you, and you will honor me" (Psalm 50:15).

I went to boot camp thinking I was close to God again. When I was in Youth Group and went to church, I wouldn't sing at all. When I was in church at boot camp, I had the urge to become at peace with God. I was away from the Drill Instructors, and I was at peace praising Him.

I have completed the hardest thing I have ever done in my life. I could not have made it through boot camp if I did not have God to count on. Of everything I learned in boot camp, this is the biggest thing: Praise God All the Time, not just when you are in trouble! God will be there and has a plan for you no matter what you think.

My son's life—his spiritual journey—on twelve index cards. This was a gift of inestimable worth.

God did answer our prayers. He protected Deryk spiritually. He grew closer to his Lord and had a greater understanding of God during the last year of his life than he'd had all the years before. God protected Deryk physically because he did not return home with loss of limbs or injuries to endure for the remainder of his life, something that would have been unbearable for him to handle. And God protected Deryk in another way, of which I'm equally thankful. Two hours into heavy battle he received a fatal shot to the left temple and immediately passed on to the presence of Jesus Christ. Deryk did not suffer in pain—his entrance into heaven was swift.

Since receiving these twelve index cards, God has opened the doors for my husband and me to give Deryk's testimony to thousands of people. We've shared his story of faith with the president of the United States and to a national group of chaplains. Over ninety people have come forward to accept Christ as a result of hearing our son's testimony, and countless brothers and sisters have rededicated their lives. Out of our sorrow has come amazing grace.

I am grateful for those who choose to serve and protect our country. I am thankful my son grew into a selfless person who cared about an oppressed people. I, along with my son, am at peace praising God. I know there will be a day when I will see Deryk again. It's what I believe, and it gives me strength.

❦ ❦ ❦

◡ *Presence of Mine Enemies* ◡

STAFF SERGEANT KEVIN FORRINGER
AS TOLD TO CYNTHIA HINKLE

MY NAME IS STAFF SERGEANT KEVIN FORRINGER. I'm a military policeman with the 307 MP Company, an Army reserve unit from New Kensington, Pennsylvania. I served in the Iraq theatre from May through Christmas Day of 2003. The story I have to tell may seem out of left field to some, as far as answered prayer goes.

I met Specialist Eric Hull in 1998 when he joined the reserves, the same year I met the other person in this story, Staff Sergeant

Mike "Mikey" Hilty. We arrived in Camp Muleskinner in May of 2003. This was located at a former Iraqi Officer's academy, where we found storage buildings full of elbow macaroni. Who'd of thought that's what those officers ate, elbow macaroni?

At Camp Muleskinner, the T-Rats, or rations, were not as good as the pasta Specialist Eric cooked with the spaghetti he and a fellow cook paid for out of their own pockets. A dozen of us lined up one evening for his tasty pasta when Eric stopped dishing up the food and called me away from the line.

"Look what my wife sent me!" the twenty-three-year-old father said, grinning.

I looked at the pictures of Eric's two little kids, all dressed up in red, white, and blue.

"Aw, they look great!" I replied, then hurried back into line as hungry soldiers glared.

Every morning and evening, our unit's teams made mail or report missions to and from Camp Muleskinner and the Battalion. We had to drive a dangerous stretch along the road to the Baghdad International Airport (BIAP). The insurgents liked to set up improvised explosive devices (IEDs) on the side of this road because they knew they would hit big military vehicles like our Humvees.

Before every mission, I'd pull out the Twenty-third Psalm card my grandfather used to carry. I read this prayer so often I knew it by heart. Then I'd say one more prayer, something like this: "Lord, protect us with Your armor, and lead us into battle with Thy sword, and guide us in doing the right things."

But I had one more prayer I added to my list in August 2003. That was the Tuesday we heard that Specialist Eric Hull's mission had encountered an IED along the road to the BIAP. I prayed most of the day for Eric until the commander told our group he didn't make it.

After Eric's death, I began to pray that God would allow us to catch the men who killed him.

One week later Staff Sergeant Mikey and I had to lead two teams on an evening mission. We had done the route thirty, maybe forty, times before. We knew the road.

For safety I knew we needed to make the round-trip before nightfall. But as we were readying to leave, we were told Mikey's driver, Specialist Stephanie "Eddie" Eddinger's foot had been stung by a bee, and it had swollen up. Another Christian friend, Sergeant Tom Cross, agreed to fill in as a driver. I was relieved we had a quick replacement.

As we mounted up and started precombat inspections, we found the radio in one of our two Humvees was not working. We delayed the mission by about ten minutes to get someone to come and fix it. After that problem was solved and we were about to get going, the other radio went down. I was really "stressing," as I knew these delays meant we would almost certainly be traveling back from Battalion in the dark.

Finally we left and I prayed.

Mikey took the lead. Suddenly his Humvee turned off the familiar route. Mikey called me and said, "I don't know why I did that. For some reason I turned off here."

I knew that wrong turn would set us back another five minutes.

When we got to Battalion, we had to drive around to the back gate because of concerns about car bombs. This extra detour slowed us up even more.

As we exited Battalion, Mikey decided to fill our water coolers with ice, a valuable commodity in Iraq. We had to stop, open the coolers, and pour ice over the bottles of water. I calculated we got slowed up another thirty minutes.

We drove back without incident...until we headed down a ramp with guardrails narrowing to a chokepoint in the road. This was the exact spot Eric had been killed the week before. Suddenly I noticed a car and two men on the side of the road. Our minds were racing.

These are the guys who killed Eric, we all thought.

Quickly we blocked the road in front of the two men. My gunner, Specialist Erik Hamza, swung the turret to the rear and trained his SAW (Squad Automatic Weapon) on the Iraqis as they quickly jumped back into their car.

As I cued my mike to tell Mikey, "Hey, what are those guys doing? Let's stop them," I saw the doors of Mikey's Humvee swing open. I turned to my driver. We both nodded in agreement and immediately dismounted.

Training our weapons on the Iraqis, we screamed, "Get out of the car!"

The men scrambled out of the car. On the car seat sat a loaded pistol and a detonator.

My team took control of the two men. Mikey and Sergeant Cross doubled back to check out the area where we saw the Iraqis fooling around on the side of the road. Within minutes, Mikey found a 150-millimeter artillery round wired to the detonator of a cordless phone. The EOD (Explosive Ordinance Division) later informed us the bomb was almost completely armed when we rolled up on the Iraqis and interrupted their work.

Once Mikey discovered the IED, we felt pretty certain these were the guys that killed our friend.

The heat was suffocating that night. We drank the cold bottled water as we held the prisoners while our base sent out an interpreter. The interpreter had to question these men at the IED site to ensure there were no other explosives set up in the area. You could call the questioning an interrogation, but these men were scared and needed very little persuasion to give up information. One of the men admitted to setting up the IED. He even admitted to setting up one exactly one week before—the one that killed Eric.

For me it was so freaky and weird that the detonator was on the seat, that they hadn't finished rigging it into place. If our team mission had delayed a few more minutes we would have been blown up.

Safely in the green zone of Baghdad, Staff Sergeant Kevin Forringer stands by the Humvee active late that August night in 2003. Ssgt. Forringer says, "You may notice that the flag is flying the wrong way on both the Humvee and my shoulder, but as you can see from my name tag, the picture is not reversed. The flag, when flown on the right shoulder (and in this case, the right side of our Humvee) will always be flown as if it were moving forward."

If our mission had not been repeatedly delayed earlier, we would not have caught these guys.

Back at the base, my friend Mikey and I stood outside the tent where the interrogation continued. A nervous wreck, I pulled out a cigarette. Unwinding I said, "You know, I gotta tell you something. It's kind of weird. Being I'm a fellow Christian, I've been praying ever since the night Eric was killed that we would catch the men who killed him.

"And you know, Mikey," I went on, "I never prayed to God to have the opportunity to kill someone. I prayed we would have the opportunity to catch them."

Staff Sergeant Mikey stared at me, his mouth dropped open.

"Kevin," he said. "I've been praying the exact same thing too—that we would have the opportunity to catch them."

Because of this capture, we caught several other men who were involved and active in the area. Later there was a raid on a house that contained bomb materials. Who knows how many attacks we may have prevented?

Our teams involved in the capture received congratulations from people higher up. The commanders felt what we did was good. They told us, "These were the men who killed your friend and yet you showed great restraint. Some guys would have probably killed them."

The night of that capture, I had a feeling of elation mixed with sadness and anger that we found these men. I tried to keep an even temper and tried to remember this happened because it was God's will. We weren't doing anything special that night; we were just doing our job. There is no doubt in my mind, nor will there ever be, that the Lord had a hand in that mission on that night. He answered my prayer, and for that I will be forever grateful.

> *This story is dedicated to Sergeant Eric Hull and Sergeant Nick Tomko, both killed in Iraq in 2004. "Greater love has no one than this, that he lay down his life for his friends"* (John 15:13).

6

Saved from Danger

Nothing moves the heart of God like the prayers of His children. This, I believe, is especially true when parents pray for their children. God understands a parent's heart—after all, He is one. And when we are helplessly far from our sons and daughters while they face danger, it's a good idea to realize we couldn't do anything better than pray even if we were right there with them. Being a parent helps us understand another facet of our heavenly Father. Lifting our children up to His Throne of Grace is better protection than any insurance policy available. He loves our kids more than we can, and He has unlimited resources to get them through the danger. This is also true when we pray for family, friends, and loved ones. In the midst of battle, there's no safer place than God's hands.

⬥⬥⬥

So Peter was kept in prison, but the church
was earnestly praying to God for him.

Acts 12:5

✌ *Miracle in the Sand* ☙

STEVEN MANCHESTER, SOMERSET, MASSACHUSETTS

Two weeks after the last shots were fired in Operation Desert Storm, I was standing at a barren traffic control point in Iraq when a lone vehicle approached. It was American, so I waved it through. The driver pulled up to me and stopped. He was a sergeant and, from the look in his eyes, he was definitely lost.

"Man, am I glad to see you!" he said with a nervous grin. "I lost my convoy in the dust storm that just passed through. I'm supposed to be on Main Supply Route Green but…"

I chuckled. The entire area was my patrol; I could have driven the roads in Iraq blindfolded.

"You're not that far off," I confirmed. "Right now, you're on Main Supply Route Blue, but this route runs parallel to Main Supply Route Green. Keep south for the next four miles or so, and when you reach a fork in the road, you've met up with Green."

The sergeant's face showed relief, and I was happy to help him. With a wave, he was on his way. I, on the other hand, returned to the boredom of the desert's miles and miles of solitary confinement.

Several unpleasant months later my platoon sergeant, Tony, and I were driving into Saudi Arabia, right through a very bad dust storm much like the one that had disoriented the sergeant. Approximately thirty miles from the border, I heard a bang.

In super slow motion, the vehicle tipped left, toward the driver's side. The windshield cracked at the top, then spidered throughout the center. As amazement swam within my eyes, the desert spun in circles, end-over-end. I felt something heavy smash into the back of my bare skull. It was an army field phone, flying around aimlessly, looking for a target. The piercing pain quickly led to numbness. My tense body went limp. I felt as if I were being submerged into a pool of warm water. Unlike any peace I had ever experienced before, the sensation was heavenly. With no choice but to accept the comfort, my eyes slammed shut. In the briefest moment in time, I watched as my life played out before me. It was a slide show, with one vivid picture after another being brought into the light.

When I finally opened my eyes, I felt pain surging throughout my body. Everything throbbed, but it was my left arm and neck that caused me to groan. Fogged from the pain and disoriented from shock, I attempted to lift my heavy head. Turning it slowly, I looked down at my fingers. The only thing missing was my wedding band. Turning right, I saw the Humvee. It was almost forty feet away, lying on its roof. It looked funny, like a helpless turtle resting on its shell. Reality struck.

It wasn't at all funny. With all my might, I pushed myself to my knees. The Humvee's motor screamed for help. It was running at full idle. Trying to clear my blurred vision, I choked on the smell of gas and oil leaking from the wreck. I took two small painful steps toward the Humvee when I saw Tony.

Like a bat, he was suspended in mid-air by his seat belt and appeared unconscious. My heart jumped into my throat and started to beat wildly. Tony was in trouble. He needed help. Picking up the pace, I ignored my own pain.

"Get out! Tony, get out!" I screamed.

Tony never moved, but the motor seemed to hear me. It raced faster. "Please, Lord, let him be okay," I prayed. Without hesitation, I dove into the Humvee. Tony was out cold. Instinctively, I unbuckled the safety belt and pulled my friend out.

A safe distance from the Humvee, I laid Tony onto the warm sand and took his pulse. The old horse was still kicking.

For a while, I just sat in the sand with Tony's head in my lap. The motor finally seized up. Tony started talking in riddles, and his shivering scared me. It was more than ninety degrees, and my friend was freezing. He was in shock. So, as the Army had trained me, I treated the symptoms accordingly. Once I'd done all I could, I returned to the Humvee to call for help.

The antenna was buried under the wreck and though I tried again and again, it was no use. Nobody heard my pleas for help. Nobody knew we existed. Everyone at base camp didn't expect us back for a whole day. There would be no search for at least that long. A helpless fear welled up inside of me. Like a stranded child searching for his parents, I called for a med-evac one last time. I waited. There was a terrible silence. With the antenna buried under the Humvee, no one could have heard my beckoning. We were alone. Fighting off despair, I grabbed my rifle, a box of ammo, and a ragged blanket, and returned to Tony. The only thing left was faith, so I knelt in the sand and prayed.

"Dear Lord, please don't let us die in this awful place. Please send us help."

Tony became more coherent and startled me with a simple question. "What in the world just happened?"

I explained the accident, adding an apology at the end.

Tony said nothing. He just grinned weakly and returned to unconsciousness.

There was nothing I could do. Traveling on foot was impossible. The radio was no longer an option. The only thing to do was wait. Sitting somewhere on the southern tip of Iraq, under a drift of powdered sugar (sand), we were in big trouble.

Time crawled by, though it was irrelevant. I sat deserted and stranded in the wild. I'd never felt so broken and alone. I sobbed in guilt, despair…even self-pity. No one should die alone.

Suddenly the hand of an angel rested upon my shoulder. Looking up, I stared into the face of the lost soldier I'd directed a few months before. I hadn't heard him approach.

The soldier bent down and gently whispered, "Lie down, Sarge. I'm gonna take care of you now. It's all over. We're gonna get you out of here." With that, he winked.

I couldn't believe it. "But how did you…" I started.

He smiled. "Nice to see you again too. After the directions you gave me, I finally found my medical unit." He looked back at the road. "I've been assigned the scout vehicle. I'm about ten minutes ahead of our convoy. They should be along in a bit."

"So how did you know we were here?" I asked. "Did you hear my radio transmission?" I knew the Humvee's antenna was buried, but there could have been no other logical explanation for his sudden appearance. At that time, in that place, it would have been a miracle for anyone to just happen by.

"What transmission?" he replied. "We were just passing through on our way back."

In awe, I collapsed onto the hot sand. My throbbing body could finally rest; my tortured mind put at ease. Catching the twinkle in the medic's saintly eyes, I believed every word he said. With all my heart, I trusted him.

Sergeant Jason Matthews, the medic, called for a chopper, and then worked feverishly. I was strapped to a long-board, while my pants and shoulder holster were completely cut off. My arm was splintered and my neck placed into a bulky brace. An IV was administered. Through it all, I slipped in and out of the real world.

Before long, the med-evac chopper flew in for the pickup. After covering me from head-to-toe with a warm foil wrap, Sergeant Matthews placed his entire upper body over my face, shielding me from the blowing sand. The incoming chopper kicked up a mountain of the powder with its giant blades. Touching down, the airborne ambulance's motor was cut down to a high-pitched whine. It was the most welcomed screech I ever heard.

Four men lifted up the canvas litter and at a sprint I was rushed into the helicopter. Looking back at Matthews, I yelled, "Thank you," though there was no way he could have ever heard me. The chopper was too loud.

With a look of urgency, though, Matthews ran over. He grabbed my hand and placed something into the palm. With a wonderful smile, he threw a thumbs-up and was gone.

I opened my hand. It was my gold wedding band, slightly deformed, but shining brightly. Goose bumps raced over my body. It was too much to be for real. But it was true. God had saved us, and we'd lived to tell about it. I slid the ring back onto my finger, and the chopper took to the air.

⛧ ⛧ ⛧

✌ A Soldier for Christ ∾

CHRISTINE TROLLINGER, KANSAS CITY, MISSOURI

MY FATHER, TOM KILDARE, was a Marine who served in the Pacific during World War II. Most of the time Dad rarely spoke about the war. Like most men who served, the subject was one with too many painful memories. Dad generally would keep the subject light and entertaining whenever he did speak about it. There was one story, though, that my father loved to tell my brothers and me whenever we would ask about the war. It was a story dear to his heart.

It happened just about the time the war was winding down and my dad was serving in the Pacific theater. One day he was assigned to scout for enemy troop movements in rough jungle terrain. He had just climbed a tree and concealed himself when out of nowhere the entire area beneath the tree was filled with enemy Japanese soldiers. Dad found himself trapped in the treetop for many hours as the enemy decided to camp right beneath the tree.

Barely able to breathe for fear of giving away his position, Dad said he spent the time praying for God's protection and asking God to help him.

Every prayer he had ever learned swirled through his mind and heart as he waited silently in that treetop. He prayed that he would not be discovered and, as time went on, he began to pray for the enemy soldiers beneath the tree. He saw in his mind's eye our family back home, and he imagined these soldiers also had loved ones they were missing too. Up close, the enemy soldiers looked just like the men in his unit. Although their language was foreign to his ears and he could not understand them, he knew deep down they were God's children, just as he was. Like him, they were ordinary men with family and friends in a country far away who might never see them again if they should die in the jungle so many miles from home.

As Dad prayed, the enemy soldiers sat relaxed and unsuspecting around the jungle clearing beneath the tree. They were laughing and sharing letters and photos from home, the same way that my dad and his fellow soldiers did when not on alert.

My father accepted that, in the end, he would probably not be returning home. The odds were stacked against him, and he knew he could not remain motionless and undetected for much longer. Having made his peace with God, my father began his final prayer. He began by praying for the soldiers beneath the tree. He prayed for their loved ones and for God's mercy on them all. He prayed for courage and most of all for forgiveness, should he be forced to begin firing. Even in the dire circumstances of war, my father did not take the commandment "Thou shalt not kill" lightly.

Just as my father gave the outcome over to our Father in heaven and made the sign of the cross, an enemy soldier spotted his hiding place in the treetop. The soldier looked directly at my dad as he made his final sign of the cross and silently said, "Amen! Thy will be done."

To his amazement, the enemy soldier silently made the sign of the cross on his own forehead, then put his finger to his lips as if to say, "Be still my brother. I shall not betray you." Almost in that very instant, the enemy forces began to move out, as silently and as quickly as they had come. My father never ceased to thank God for

His protection that day. He also never forgot to pray for his brother soldier of Christ, whose name he never knew. His brother, who saved his life because both of them loved God, who loved them both equally.

❦ ❦ ❦

✎ On Empty ✎

COMMANDER JESSE S. CLEVELAND (USN RET.)
AS TOLD TO HIS DAUGHTER GINGER COX, GAFFNEY, SOUTH CAROLINA

Train a child in the way he should go, and when he is old he will not turn from it (Proverbs 22:6).

WITH A WARNING LIGHT in my cockpit shining brightly, my Hellcat sped above the endless waves of the western Pacific Ocean. The light had appeared just moments after I completed my first attack run. Now I anxiously searched the horizon for the Task Force. Would I reach a carrier in time? In a flash of comic relief, I thought, *Thank goodness Dad can't see me now!*

I was born and raised far from the ocean, on a ranch ten miles north of Cisco, Texas. My parents, having a large family, worked long hard days and expected the same from their children. When not at school, I was busy working in the fields and pastures.

During the midthirties, US Army Air Corps planes frequently passed over our place on training flights. The young pilots often flew at treetop level—so low I could see flashing eyes framed by goggles and broad grins above white scarves that waved from the cockpits.

Watching these young pilots spurred my passion to fly. At night in my room I sent off requests for anything I could find on aviation.

I visited the local airstrip and watched air shows staged by "barn-storm pilots." And I occasionally got aboard for a quick flight without my father's knowledge. Since a neighbor's son had died in a plane crash, Dad would not have given permission for me to ride in one. Nevertheless, I would sneak flights whenever I got a chance.

When the Japanese attacked Pearl Harbor on December 7, 1941, I was attending a small church college in Bethany, Oklahoma. The US Navy announced it needed young men in its new aviation cadet-training program (V-5), and I immediately applied. While waiting for active duty, I earned a private pilot's license through the Civilian Pilot Training (CPT) program. I aced the grueling physical endurance tests for active service—thanks to my conditioning on our farm. My passion for flying pushed me through a series of training programs in various aircraft.

After finishing advanced training, I was designated a naval aviator and awarded the "Navy Wings of Gold." Then came operational flight training in the F4F "Wildcat" fighter. Near the Great Lakes area, I learned to land on two converted coal carriers, Wolverine and Sable. Dubbed "The Cisco Kid," I proudly met every challenge the Navy threw at me.

Ready for assignment to fleet duty, I reported to Pearl Harbor as a replacement pilot. The Fighting Squadron One

The "Cisco Kid," Commander Jesse S. Cleveland (USN)—" 'God, please look after me and the other pilots.' With that brief prayer, a calm assurance swept over me, filling me with an inner strength."

Operations Officer took me to a new F6F "Hellcat" saying, "Cisco, I know you haven't flown one of these yet, but here is a manual. Climb in the cockpit and look it over."

Following three quick hours of flight time in the Hellcat, the Navy transferred me to Fighting Squadron Thirty, which was returning to combat in the South Pacific. After only two practice carrier landings near Pearl Harbor, I departed aboard the *USS Monterey* for the combat area. Fortunately I managed a couple more takeoffs and landings before we reached our destination, Palau Island, off the west of the Mariana Islands (Guam, Saipan, and Tinian).

Our Air Group Commander briefed us before our first mission: "Gentlemen, you have three jobs this morning. First, get out there and destroy aircraft in the air and on the ground. Second, destroy antiaircraft positions, hangars, and ammo-fuel storage facilities. Drop your belly tanks on their hangar areas so your 50-caliber incendiary ammunition can ignite it. And third, get you and your plane safely back here for the next mission."

After an early morning launch, we rendezvoused with other aircraft and headed for the target area. Suddenly reality hit. This attack mission was for real. My life or death could depend on how well I did my job. I was to seek and destroy. Today would I be facing an enemy pilot with the same orders?

My thoughts soared across thousands of miles to our Texas ranch, across the years to my childhood in a loving Christian home. My mother and father worked hard and prayed often for their children. Five of my brothers were in military service—one each in the Marine and Army Air Corps, one on a naval battleship, and two in the U.S. Army. More brothers would follow. I knew that not only family, but also church friends were anxiously praying for us.

In growing up, church attendance had been a painful experience. My brothers and I sat rigid each Sunday on the worn wooden pew, forced to hear hellfire and damnation sermons. The preacher would shout, pound the pulpit, and point his accusing fingers straight at us.

Although relieved when the services ended, I was continually reminded I was a prime candidate for hell. I believed in God, but those sermons kept me from wanting to get anywhere close to Him.

But as I flew straight toward the enemy, I felt a real emptiness. I wanted the strong faith that my father and mother had. I needed help and found myself pleading, "God, please look after me and the other pilots." With that brief prayer, a calm assurance swept through me, filling me with an inner strength.

Arriving at the target area, we were greeted by heavy antiaircraft fire but, thankfully, no air opposition. We made a strafing run on the "AAA positions" and aircraft on the ground. As instructed, I dropped the belly tank on the first of six runs. The attack was soon over. Mission accomplished!

It was then I noticed my "Low Fuel" warning light flash on. "Hank," I called over the radio to the division leader. "I've got a low fuel state."

"We'll head straight for the Task Group," he replied. Then calling *USS Monterey,* he advised them, "My wing man has a low fuel state. Try to get him a straight-in approach."

As I banked the Hellcat into a U-turn and scrambled back toward the carrier, I suddenly realized my potentially fatal error. I had left the ship using the fuel in my internal tank that was supposed to be for my return. The belly tank, which I should have used in flying to the target, had still been full when I dropped it.

Now flying on fumes, over miles and miles of whitecaps beckoning me, I finally sighted the Task Force. Thankfully, the carriers were into the wind. Making a straight-in approach, I landed with the fuel gauge arrow flat on "Empty." My first combat mission had ended at last…empowered by prayer.

By the end of my first combat tour, I completed 116 more missions. Prayers were as important as preflight checks during my twenty-six years of flying in the U.S. Navy.

Ground combat troops had a saying; "There is no such thing as an atheist in a foxhole." And I can tell you for a fact, there was also no atheist in my Hellcat—just a newly enlisted prayer warrior.

> But those who hope in the LORD will renew their strength.
> They will soar on wings like eagles (Isaiah 40:31).

꙳ ꙮ ꙳

◌ The Hand of God ◌

LEROY "PETE" PETERSON
AS TOLD TO TRICIA GOYER, KALISPELL, MONTANA

THERE ARE MANY MEMORIES OF WAR that last a lifetime. Memories of buddies lost right before one's eyes, of prisoners, of battles. Sometimes these memories meet me at the strangest times, but there's one memory above all that has changed me forever.

Bastogne and the Battle of the Bulge was no picnic. I was wounded there, and I remember sixty years ago as if it were yesterday. Our unit had been corralled in a low area. I was a medic, and this is where we'd based our headquarters.

As a medic, you go where you're needed. One day we received a radio message. They were desperate for medics in the next town. The infantry had taken severe punishment, and they'd lost two medical men who'd been shot.

My medical officer approached me. "Come on, Pete, we've got to move out."

I said goodbye to a couple of good buddies, radio operators I was talking to, and jumped into the jeep. The driver, with Major Harold

G. Stacy beside him and me in the back, headed off. To get to the next town we had to cross a high point, a very high point. We didn't know it at the time, but the Germans had this area pegged with their big 88 guns.

As we hit the top of that hill, a gun shell went over us. It landed about fifty feet away—at the very most. The next one landed right in front of us. We knew we had to abandon ship. The major jumped out one side, and I dove out the other. On my side of the road I spotted the slightest gully, and into it I jumped.

I knew I had little protection and figured I was a goner since the Germans were firing from my side. I quickly asked the Lord to save my life. Then something amazing happened. As I lay there, I felt someone pushing on my back, pushing me deeper into the ground and telling me to get down.

Rounds three, four, and five landed on the jeep. Soon there was nothing left of it. But as I lay in that ditch, I had a sensation of protection—one I'll never forget. I was thankful for whoever was on top of me, protecting me from the brunt of the fallout.

When it was over, blood dripped from my nose and ears. The major was okay, but I had concussion problems from the shells that shook the ground. As I slowly got up, it was clear no one had been on top of me—at least no earthly being.

It took five days of rest before I could resume my duties. And even though I looked fine on the outside, something had changed within.

I'd been a Christian since I was a small child, but my faith grew after feeling the protection of the Lord pressing upon me. I'm still a strong Christian today because of that experience. Many people can deny God exists, but not me. I've felt His hand—His entire body in fact—and I've heard His whisper in the midst of war. And I'll never again be the same.

◡ *My Only Son* ◠

REVEREND PATRICIA DUNCAN, CLINTON, MARYLAND

THE CLOCK TICKED LOUDLY against the silence of the night. *Two in the morning—that's all?* I thought, as I pulled the covers over my head. But buried beneath my blankets I heard another deafening sound—my own heartbeat racing the persistent ticking of the clock.

"It's a peace mission, Mom. I'll be fine, but I have to go."

And I released my only son to accomplish his patriotic duty.

"He who dwells in the shelter of the Most High will rest in the shadow of the Almighty...." I repeated Psalm 91 over and over, but I found no solace in the comforting words of Scripture that night.

I jumped out of bed and screamed into the night, "Why, Lord? Couldn't you have stopped the orders? Why does Gart have to be in Bosnia now? He's my only son!" I cried.

I thought back many years ago, to when Gart's father was killed during the Vietnam War. Our son was only five years old. Smiling through my tears, I remembered the night I told him that his daddy was in heaven. I thought Gart would be terrified, but instead he answered, "Mom, I'm the man of the house now."

I saluted him. "Yes, Sir." But then I asked him, "Who will take care of the man of the house, Sir?"

"God will, Mommy. God will."

His words echoed through my fearful heart. God was taking care of my son in Bosnia. I was sure of that now, so I went back to bed. This time I fell into a calm and peaceful sleep.

The next morning I arrived at the office around 8:00, just in time for our morning prayer meeting. Just as I was going in, I heard one of my co-workers praying for my son. Everyone knew he had been in Bosnia nearly a year now, but no one had ever prayed so fervently before.

Later that night, I received a call from my Gart. He was sobbing.

"Gart, what's wrong?"

"Mom, I came close to getting killed."

I gasped as he continued, "I was getting medical supplies when suddenly I was attacked. There were several men with rifles, and one was placed at my temple ready to fire. I started praying, Mom, and they suddenly ran as if they had seen a ghost…but I was the only one in the room. As they ran, some soldiers from my company spotted them and shot the tires of their vehicles and captured them." He was quiet for a moment. "Mom, I believe God must have sent His angels to protect me."

I cried tears of joy, and I told him about my co-worker's prayer. He said the incident occurred at what just happened to be 8:00 our time—the exact moment the prayer was being offered for my son.

After that, I never doubted or complained about Gart's tour in Bosnia because it was evident: God was taking care of my son—the man of the house. God had covered him with His protection, and I am forever grateful.

7
Family Ties

Some of us grew up in Christian homes and attended church every time the doors were open. Others may have barely frequented a church and cannot begin to relate. The same holds true for military families. Even things such as the Pledge of Allegiance and Veteran's Day hold a deeper meaning civilians can only imagine. Figuring in the military's take with every family decision becomes a way of life; in many ways, this is a sacrifice taken for granted by nonmilitary families who reap the rewards in their freedoms, with little understanding of the cost. Military families are often like trees in a storm—standing strong with roots firmly planted, yet flexible enough so as not to break when bitter winds blow.

⋆⋆⋆

*These commandments that I give you today are to be upon
your hearts. Impress them on your children. Talk about them
when you sit at home and when you walk along the road,
when you lie down and when you get up. Tie them as symbols
on your hand and bind them on our foreheads. Write them
on the doorframes of your houses and on your gates.*

DEUTERONOMY 6:6-9

↭ Into a Hot, Lonely Place ↭

SHAWN M. HELGERSON, FAIRCHILD AIR FORCE BASE, WASHINGTON

THERE IS AN AIR FORCE SAYING that goes, "The two best bases in the world are the one you're going to and the one you just left." Edwards Air Force Base had been rough for Jackie and me. Fairchild held hope for the future. After two weeks at our new base, my commander came to my desk. "Sergeant Helgerson," she said, "I need you to go to the desert with me."

A team from another base was short a few bodies, and they needed us to fill in. President Bush was talking about going into Iraq, and my heart sank with the question.

"How long?" I asked.

"At least one hundred seventy-nine days. But there's no way to tell at this point. It could be as much as a year."

My heart sank a little more. "I'm sorry, Ma'am. I meant, how long do I have to get ready?"

"Let's see," she said, "It's Tuesday morning, and we're leaving on Saturday. Four days."

"I'll be ready," I said.

The next four days were a blur of briefings, appointments, training, and tears. Jackie and I had long discussions deep into the night about all the hows, whys, and what ifs of going to the desert. I tried to allay her fears, but mine were as deep as hers.

"This is what I signed up for, Jackie. We know this is part of military life."

"I just don't see why it has to be you. Why can't someone else go?"

"Everyone has to go eventually," I said, "This is why we get paid the big bucks."

She laughed a little through her tears.

It was 4 AM and the cab was waiting outside. Jackie threw her skewed hair up in a makeshift ponytail. She wore my bathrobe and held a big mug of coffee. I kissed my sleeping stepdaughter and rubbed her eyebrows and cheek with my thumb. My youngest son lay sprawled in his crib, chubby legs exposed and binky dangling from his mouth. As I kissed his face and squeezed his fat thigh, it occurred to me I was going to miss his first birthday, his first steps, maybe his first words. For the first time, tears fell from my eyes and a sob escaped my throat.

The cab driver tossed my bags in the trunk while I said goodbye to Jackie. Tears flowed freely down her face, and she held me tightly until it hurt.

"I have to go."

"Hurry, I don't want you to remember me like this. I'm a mess."

"No, Babe, all our best times together you looked like this. I've seen you bring babies into the world, and you were beautiful then. You've never been more beautiful to me. I'm the only one who gets to see this look. It's exactly how I want to remember you." I pulled out my camera and snapped a picture. She tried to smile.

I held both her hands in mine and said, "Let's pray."

"Precious Father," I prayed, "Jackie and I don't know what the future holds and, Lord, we're scared. This is such a huge step for both of us. But we know You are in control, Lord, and we put our trust in You. Give us Your strength, Lord. Keep us safe while we're apart. And Lord, let our love grow stronger always. Amen."

Jackie's eyes glistened and the lump in my throat ached.

"Goodbye," we both said, and I kissed her one last time. I walked across the snowy yard and we drove away.

A month passed and I made little progress toward the Middle East. I met with my team from McConnell Air Force Base in Kansas, but we were stuck. President Bush hadn't announced we were going into Iraq yet; Turkey hesitated to let American troops into their country for fear of Muslim retaliation; military flights heading overseas were either full or broken. So we sat at McConnell, played pool, read, and drank beer. I spent time in my room, at the gym, or at the library e-mailing Jackie.

President Bush announced we were going to Iraq on St. Patrick's Day. Two weeks later I was in Saudi Arabia waiting for a ride to Iraq. It was my first trip to the Middle East, and the desolation was dumbfounding. My first real pains for Jackie set in. I had been away from her for a week here or a day there, but never for this much time and never so far. The distance and starkness made the loneliness more intense.

Finally it was Kirkuk, Iraq. We got off the plane and flames licked the sky all around the base. A firefight the night before left everyone jumpy with nerves on edge. The commander warned us to stay on the beaten path. Some Iraqi bodies still lay in their bunkers and were likely booby-trapped. He assured us the Army would clear them soon.

The first night I slept with my rifle—a clip in and the safety off. We slept in an abandoned dorm building—no guard on duty, no perimeter security. The Army was there before us and tore the place apart. Looters came before the Army. Concrete debris, trash, and human and animal feces filled the rooms. Fear and uncertainty filled the rooms too, as thickly as the dust.

Over the next few months we rebuilt, rewired, replumbed, put up tents, laid out roads, and constructed buildings to make the base operational. The sun baked us mercilessly, boiled our drinking water, and bleached our clothes. Heat waves rolled off the hills. Scorpions raised their bodies off the hot earth, and camel spiders leapt at us from the fields. At night gunfire kept us awake until we learned to sleep with our helmets and flak jackets on.

Eventually we called it home: "I'm going home to sleep" or "I can't wait to get home and take off these boots." Much the same way a businessman comes to call his hotel room home after a while.

But it isn't home—can never be home. A trip to the desert is like our time on earth. We are spiritual beings on an earthly journey rather than earthly beings on a spiritual journey. Yet we get attached to this place. The fact we have to leave saddens and scares us. It was the same way in the desert. A few friends left early—some went home to the States; some gave their lives. We miss them all. We should have been happy for the ones who went home early, but their absence hurt. Still, we had to wait our turns, regardless of how we felt.

When my day came, I was over the moon. A couple days' travel, and I'd be in the arms of my wife. A civilian can never understand the joy a military member feels seeing family after so long. Months of waiting, working, and yearning are finally over. There are no more bullets whizzing overhead, no more worrying about perimeter security. In that moment there is only the warm embrace of family, the sweet smell of your wife, the soft touch of your children's hands.

Jackie was everything I anticipated. After all those months, she was more beautiful than I remembered. Her kiss more tender, her embrace sweeter, her love more satisfying than I dreamed of all those nights away. I lifted her off the ground and squeezed her until my fingers tingled. "I love you," I said again and again and swung her around.

"God answered our prayers, Shawn. I knew He would. I knew you'd come home safe. I prayed every day."

My youngest son was walking—running really. I squeezed him hard, and he took my scruffy face in his little hands. My stepdaughter bounded into my arms and refused to let go of my neck.

It will be a perfect day, untainted by earthly sorrows and mistakes, that day we get to see Jesus, bow down to worship at His feet, and finally feel that perfect love of which our earthly loves are only a shadow. I imagined this is how it might be when we get to heaven.

∾ One More Night ∾

RONA CUNNINGHAM, NORTHPORT, ALABAMA

It's HARD TO POINT OUT just one of the many times during my husband's year-long tour where God especially touched our family. There has been an abundance of God's grace all along the journey, at home, and in Afghanistan. As we have prayed with faith, there is one particular memory that renews us and reminds us our prayers are always answered.

It was December when Dwayne's Army Reserve unit was put on active duty. He would be preparing to leave us to serve our country in Afghanistan for the next year. Daily my husband was driving two-and-a-half hours each way to Huntsville to join his unit and prepare for deployment. After a few weeks of traveling, the day finally arrived; it was time for goodbyes.

We drove him to the ceremony and knew this time he wouldn't be returning home with us. Through the hurt, we understood the Lord had a hand in even this…this unbelievable day. After thirteen years of marriage and ten years of fatherhood, we would walk without him for a year. After a special, heart-touching ceremony to honor these brave soldiers, the time had come to say goodbye… well, so we thought.

The captain had everyone ready and all things were in line. He then said the soldiers could have another night off…if they had transportation to return by the next morning. We were so excited and so exhausted! We had built up for goodbyes and were now blessed with a few more hours and one more night at home. We wanted to savor every last touch, smile, and laugh, and yet the sobering thought of the clock still ticking was among us.

As we were leaving Huntsville, driving home to Tuscaloosa, we passed the Space and Rocket Center. All three of our children asked to go see the huge rockets in the sky. We stopped in hopes we could just walk around to glance at the rockets. After entering the center, we realized we would have to purchase tickets just to look at the rockets. We couldn't afford this expense, so we told the kids we would visit another time. They had a very understanding look as we turned to go out the doors. As we were leaving, an employee noticed my husband's uniform and asked him if he was deploying or returning. After a brief update, the employee asked if we were going through the center.

Dwayne replied politely that we stopped to get a glance at the rockets but were not prepared to go through the center. The man asked us to wait a moment and returned with five passes for the entire center and Imax theatre. We were shocked and very excited to be blessed with this turn in events. This man saw the excitement on our children's faces and the gratitude in our eyes. He gave us a chance to forget about the goodbyes and disappointments and focus on family and fun. As we entered the center, we gathered our children to explain to them God's hand in this. We thanked the Lord and prayed for this man to be blessed by his actions because of the blessing we had received. After hours of fun, learning, laughs, and memories we confirmed, "This is the day the Lord hath made," and we did rejoice in it.

Little did I know what else the Lord had in store for us. After the Space and Rocket Center, we stopped by a PX to buy a few things my husband could add to his supplies. While shopping around, our ten-year-old daughter came up and hugged me.

With a very sober look, she said," Momma, I feel weird."

I asked, "Are you okay? Are you sick?"

She replied, "No, I just don't know how to explain this."

She reminded me of how our family had prayed together the night before. After she went to bed, she'd prayed again. This time she asked for one more night with her daddy. She wanted me to know that's why the captain let him off and that's why he was with us.

All I could do was hug her tight and hold back the tears. I reassured her that she shouldn't feel weird or doubt what the Lord had done. I told her He had answered her prayer and to remember this day.

She looked up and said, "I just wish I would have asked for him not to go at all!"

Oh, what a thought! As we talked, I told her the Lord knew her daddy needed to go and He had prepared us for his leaving. The Lord will answer our prayers of protection for him, and us, in the coming year. The Lord didn't put it on her heart to ask for him not to go, but He gave her faith to believe we could have one more night. Praise God for her testimony and faith in our Lord and Savior.

My husband has safely returned home as I write this story a year later, yet the emotions are still there. We have remembered this prayer many times since it was answered. We just have to remember to see the Lord in all things, especially in being given just "one more night."

❧ ❧ ❧

∽ The Locket ∼

CARLETA GOODWIN FERNANDES, AMARILLO, TEXAS

"MY DEAREST JOHN, the baby was born on the ninth of this month, and I have named her Carleta Jon. I hope you are pleased she is named after you."

So began a letter dated November 15, 1940, to twenty-three-year-old Private First Class John Beavers, Marines 5th Fleet Force, stationed as an American Embassy guard in Peping, now Beijing,

China. The letter was from my mother, Myrtle Beavers Goodwin, to her younger, and favorite, brother.

John was pleased to hear the news, and on his next leave out of the embassy compound, he bought a present for his new niece. It was a small white-gold locket crested with an enameled flower.

On a whim, John pinned the locket to his undershirt, beneath his uniform. After a time it became a habit, and he continued to wear it there. As he prayed nightly, the locket was a soothing reminder of home, family, and friends so very far away.

December 7, 1941, two hours before the bombing of Pearl Harbor, enemy forces surrounded the embassy. Superior officers ordered the guards to surrender. Without a shot being fired, John and about thirty others were now prisoners of war.

John's parents, Albert and Lillian Beavers, were notified: John was missing.

Tensing, China, became the unpleasant home to the captives for almost two years. Late in 1943 the Japanese moved the prisoners by boat to Japan. An American airplane fired on the craft—miraculously all escaped injury. Though some of the prisoners were separated, John and several others worked together as slave laborers in the steel mills of Tokyo. American airplanes strafing the mills forced the Japanese to move their captives to the mountains.

From December 7, 1941, until mid-1944, John's family was unsure of his fate. They knew only of the capture. Myrtle continued to write letters to her brother and prayed that John was alive to get them.

Early in 1944, the Japanese allowed John and several other POWs to record messages to their families in the USA. The recordings aired in New York on April 21, 1944.

Several kind souls heard and forwarded John's message to his parents.

A printed card John's dad, Albert received read, in part, "Dear Dad, I am as well as can be expected and hope you are doing as good as you look in the pictures Myrtle sent me. I received two letters from

Myrtle and two from Betty Sue (a niece) since I have been here in Japan. I received one from you in Shanghai. Send me a food box if you will, about one every two months. This is PFC John Beavers, formerly of Peping, China, wishing the family a happy Easter. I wish to add, also, to the Japanese for allowing me to send this message, thanks."

John was alive. God heard the prayers of his family.

After my mother's death, I found two warped recordings of this message among her belongings. I gave the damaged discs to my cousin Sam, John's son. He, in turn, donated them to the Texas Tech Museum in Lubbock, Texas. The museum staff is working to restore them so once again the voices of these POWs will be heard.

Throughout the ordeal of captivity, John managed to keep the little locket hidden from his tormentors, knowing the punishment would be severe if it were found. The locket was the only personal item he managed to keep. It continually reminded him of home and the family waiting for him.

The answer to John's prayers finally came in late 1945. In a prisoner exchange, the Japanese released him to the United States. Prior to his honorable discharge from the Marines at the Naval Air Technical Training Center (NATTC) in Norman, Oklahoma, he endured several weeks of medical checkups before finally being reunited with his loved ones.

I was almost seven years old when John finally gave me the gift he'd bought years before. It was many more years before I realized the true value of what the locket stood for in terms of the testing of faith, suffering, and degradation.

Since I was a child who lost or broke everything I got close to, my mother chose to put the locket away until I could appreciate and care for it.

I married, began to raise a family, and seldom thought about the locket until 1961, when Uncle John came to visit. I wanted to show him I still had the little gift he had gone through so much to bring back to me. I went to my jewelry box. It was gone. Near tears, I wondered, *Where is it?*

My son's school was getting ready for a Halloween carnival. His teacher had asked parents to donate jewelry and small trinkets for their booth as prizes. With the help of four small children, I'd gathered several items, many from my meager collection of costume and junk jewelry. Did we accidentally include the locket?

The next morning I called the school and explained the problem. I told the principal the history and gave him a description. I prayed the locket was not gone. "Please look through the donations," I begged. "It just has to be there."

Later that day a teacher called back, "I don't believe we have it. There is a large amount of jewelry and such, but I found nothing like what you are missing. I'm so sorry."

Now I was in tears. If the locket was in with the other items, and someone did win it at the Halloween carnival, it would appear worthless. The locket was lost.

Nine years passed. One afternoon I was babysitting my friend's two year old, Gina. She liked nothing better than playing in my jewelry box. My "jewels" were few and of little value. Letting her play with them usually meant several hours of entertainment for one busy girl.

Gina turned the little black box over, dumping the contents onto a low table where she played. The shallow bottom drawer fell out. When I tried to replace it, it wouldn't fit. Something was wedged in the back. There in the back, hidden for so long, was my locket. The tears I shed were now tears of joy.

In 1976 I was living in Leavenworth, Kansas. I kept the locket near, but would never wear it for fear of loss. The rod holding the heart shape to the drop bar was gone and the locket was being precariously held together with a bent pin. A friend of mine from Fort Leavenworth was a part-time jeweler. I asked him to replace the pin, extracting a promise that he would guard the locket closely. He agreed and took the locket to his shop.

The next weekend there was a burglary at my house. Among the things taken was my little black jewelry box. If I hadn't let my friend take the locket to repair it... But the locket was safe, and it was returned to me a few days later. It was repaired and once again in my possession, where it still is today, locked away in my household safe.

John passed away on April 6, 2002, at age 85, after serving his country in the military and service to the world with almost twenty-five years as an agronomist with the United Nations.

The locket is something I will always treasure. Countless prayers, answered and unanswered, are locked within its fragile casing. It reminds me of the tremendous sacrifices many of the men and women of our military have paid for our freedom. And how an armor of prayer can see us through.

ॐ ॐ ॐ

↭ Air Force Brat ↮

C. Hope Clark, Phoenix, Arizona

Growing up on military bases in the 1960s, we "brats" shared the same bond as our fathers, who were devoted to careers protecting democracy and world peace. We shared the roar of B-52s on Strategic Air Command Air Force Base flight lines, and we shared the same realization that at any moment an "alert" would scramble our fathers to their positions in response to a world emergency. We knew the Pledge of Allegiance from the time we could talk, and we said it with fervor.

Military families were very close, and together we held our collective breath when orders came through for the Southeast Asia assignments. One year seemed forever for children while dads did their tours and moms held families together. Many mothers struggled with the load of temporary single parenthood, but military families had each other.

Our family enjoyed the luxury of our dad's presence longer than most. Feeling quite lucky in this regard, I became complacent in the knowledge that my dad hadn't received any menacing orders—until 1969, when Dad announced his orders for Danang, South Vietnam.

Daddy's job as an NCO in fuels maintenance didn't place him on the front line, but it certainly didn't completely remove him from harm's way. The Viet Cong shelled bases frequently, and fuel was volatile. Vietnam's name meant danger in any capacity, at any locale, and the country's soil was contaminated with fear and instability.

I was the eldest of two sisters and possessed a particular closeness to my dad. In my eyes, Daddy stood tall and strong, like Superman, able to stop any bullet. When he left, the ache in my heart matched nothing I'd ever experienced in my teenage life. I groped for balance and sought comfort the entire time, never finding the peace I desperately needed.

Mom tried but never quite filled the void left by Daddy. I remember how she held tightly to my hand as her husband—my daddy—boarded the plane to leave. Her tears dropped on my fingers, but I never heard her weep. Her strength was comforting, but nothing could replace the emptiness I felt as I watched his plane fly out of sight.

The television bombarded us each evening with the six o'clock news. Few households were exempt from the torment of knowing at least one person who had been killed, injured, traumatized, or was missing. The list of casualties scrolled slowly down the screen, and though we knew we'd be contacted before seeing a loss broadcast to

USAF Staff Sergeant David M. Beales, Jr.—"For one year, my daddy had existed on another continent, but at least I knew he still lived in my world. After a year of holding emotions in check, I let down my guard and cried," said Sgt. Beales' daughter, C. Hope Clark.

the country, we still held our breath until the alphabetical listing passed our family's initial.

Daddy wrote Mom daily, and once a week my sister and I would receive a letter of our own. Gifts of jade, teak, and bronze arrived frequently along with photos of GIs posing in barracks, planes, and jeeps. In turn, we packaged sweets and treats for our dad, his buddies, and the Vietnamese orphans located near the base. One photo showed Daddy alongside a soldier sporting a head bandage. For one horrific moment, we envisioned rifle fire, bombs, shrapnel, and grenades—until we read the caption stating he had fallen out of his bunk.

Finally the year drew to a close. Mom took my sister and me shopping for the perfect fashions. When Daddy came home, he was going to see three exquisite, stunning ladies. Mom spent $100 on a pantsuit, a healthy price tag in 1970. Everything was ready.

We were anxiously awaiting confirmation of his arrival back in the States when the phone call came. A plane carrying troops returning from Danang crashed into the sea shortly after takeoff, but the identifications of the injured and dead remained unconfirmed. The authorities told us someone would be in touch as soon as possible. In shock, we waited for the phone to ring again, but dreaded it as well.

For one year, my daddy had existed on another continent, but at least I knew he still lived in my world. After a year of holding emotions in check, I let down my guard and cried. How could a loving God protect him from bullets yet allow him to die on the way back home? Locking myself in my room, I prayed, soaking my pillow with tears, begging the Lord Almighty to bring Daddy home. Never before had prayer seemed so crucial, so vital.

The phone rang, and my blood chilled for a moment. The plane that crashed had preceded my dad's flight, and he was en route to us at that very moment. Agony was replaced by a rushing thrill made all the more extraordinary by the scare.

Daddy retired at the age of forty, with twenty-two years of service under his belt. I recall the pomp and circumstance of his retirement ceremony. It was a breezy, warm December midday, 1974, on Charleston Air Force Base. In his Dress Blues, under a color-coordinated cloudless sky, he received commendation for his military service. I beamed, watching him march, halt, and crisply salute. Proud not only of him, but of the loyalty, dedication, and service he represented, I watched this chapter of our lives close. Recalling the people and places, the opportunities and experiences, the pride and the responsibilities, I deduced that now and forevermore, I was and will continue to be an Air Force brat. And once again I prayed, thanking God for being in control.

☞☜☞

∽ *Quest for Carl* ∼

JUDY SPOLARICH, SACRAMENTO, CALIFORNIA

I SCRUNCHED DOWN INTO MY COAT as bitter wind whipped about my face. The countless white crosses and deafening silence overwhelmed me as tears slipped down my face. I pleaded with God, "Why do I have this burning desire to find him? Why have you placed this heavy burden upon my heart? If you want me to find him, please show me the way. This seems so hopeless. How can I find him among so many graves, in such a lonely place?"

In the distance, I spied a lone man walking toward me. "Lord, is he here for me?" He passed me. *I guess not.* Suddenly he turned and called out, "Are you an American? Are you looking for someone?" Yes. The French caretaker of the Brittany American Cemetery and Memorial became an instant answer to prayer. Signaling my husband, Gary, we walked toward the visitor's center as I shared what little I knew about my great-uncle's death.

I did not learn of Carl's story until ten years after my father's death. One day as I taxed Grandma's long-term memory banks with queries about her family, she casually mentioned her youngest brother died sometime after D-Day and was buried in France.

Most of the information the family learned about Carl came from fellow comrades in arms. Carl was a tank driver, TEC 4, and lost his first tank in the heat of battle. Undaunted, he commandeered another tank until it was mistakenly destroyed by "friendly fire." With little funds available for a burial, Great-grandma Kolb opted to let her youngest child remain with the thousands of other fallen heroes resting in France.

Dad had also been stationed in England during the war and had been a master sergeant in the Army Air Corps. He first caught gunner assignment on a B-17, the Flying Fortress, as he was the only fellow small enough to squeeze into the cubbyhole. Later he manned the radio on the famed flyer. Over the years he shared adventures and exploits, including stories of England, her sites, and her people. So why had Dad never mentioned his Uncle Carl?

From the time I first heard Carl's story, it seemed as though a mission had been laid upon my heart to find his final resting place. Once we planned our visit to France, I searched the Internet for possible burial sites. I kept my plans hidden from everyone except Gary. Yet I did not reveal to him the full weight lying upon my heart. For the most part, I did not understand the burden myself.

Through answered prayer, the compassionate French caretaker found Carl's name listed among the records. Carl was not at Brittany; instead, we learned he rested in the G Section at Normandy. Assailed by hugs and tears of joy, the gentleman received my heartfelt thanks. Gary and I continued our search the next day after spending a peaceful night on Mont St. Michelle.

The site of so many white crosses and Stars of David at Brittany was overwhelming, yet I could barely contain the raw emotions I faced when I saw the panoramic view of the thousands who rest at Normandy. Jesus' words echoed in my head, "Greater love has no one than this, that he lay down his life for his friends" (John 15:13). These men and women had done just that. It hit me that we were not just visiting Carl, but all those who lay before us. They gave their lives for our country, our allies' countries, fellow soldiers, families, friends, and even strangers. The awesome privilege of standing in such a hallowed place was truly a blessing from God.

We found Carl fairly close to the end of a row containing hundreds of graves. I cried and thanked God for the honor of being the first in my family to find him. After posing for photos, I stood next to his grave, silently introducing myself and praying over the site. The humbling power of prayer was evident as peace washed over me. I found him. We found him.

Celebrating Grandma's birthday nearly two weeks later, I presented her with a framed photo of me standing next to Carl's alabaster cross. I am not sure Grandma fully understood whose cross I stood next to or where the picture had been shot, but the rest of our family was thrilled with the story. I shared with them the odd feeling of standing on American soil while still in France and the incredible beauty of the cemeteries.

It was then that my uncles, my father's brothers, shared another story with me.

"Did you know Carl was killed by friendly fire?" they asked.

"Yes, I knew that."

"Did you know it was your dad's squadron that fired down on him?"

The revelation took some time to digest, and I was speechless. According to my uncles, the family eventually received details surrounding Carl's death from fellow troops who served with him. Through those snippets of information, Dad pieced the puzzle together. Dad's squadron had indeed fired upon Carl's tank, and Dad had flown a mission over the area that same day.

It all made sense now. No wonder my Dad had never mentioned Carl. We all know that through the fog of war mistakes happen, lives are unintentionally lost, and soldiers suffer remorse. Dad committed his life to Christ only a couple of years before his death in 1982. I thank God that during those final years, Dad knew that

Judy Spolarich's "quest for Carl" ends at a Normandy cemetery.

he could place the burdens of any human guilt onto a loving, heavenly Father, who knows all and understands every emotion.

A few years have passed, and Grandma is no longer with us. Carl is no longer lost to us, although it took half a century to find him. He was a part of our family, someone we missed, though we never knew him. The experience enriched my life and still stirs deep emotion within me. I am certain God sent me on this journey. It brought me closer to Dad. I believe that in some way I completed an unfinished chapter in my father's life.

When I gaze upon the photo of me standing by the white cross, I have a sense of fulfillment, an answer to prayer. How many of my family members had prayed for and about Carl? I know I had. God convicted me with the desire to find him. Not knowing why, I trusted the Lord to lead me to him. He did, and I am grateful for the honor of being sent on the quest for Carl. In spirit, Carl returned to California in the heart of a grand-niece. He and Dad both rest here with me, in my heart.

🐦 🐦 🐦

✌ God Said Yes ✌

LINDA MAE BALDWIN, BREMERTON, WASHINGTON

You NEED TO BE THERE for the laying of the keel, not the launching of the ship, Boy." The Navy Commander glared at my young Marine Corps lance corporal husband before denying the requested emergency/maternity leave. He was in Okinawa, Japan, and I was living with my new in-laws in the States. I was only eighteen, alone, scared, and I wanted my husband home with me. Lance and I were high school sweethearts. We graduated and went straight to Vegas, getting married at 9:00 PM in the Candlelight Wedding Chapel on the famous Strip. At our engagement announcement, my sister-in-law proclaimed that our marriage wouldn't last three years before it was over. I was determined to hold the union together past that.

Yet in only a matter of months, our marriage was in trouble. Two months into it, we fought constantly and sometimes physically. We had no support from home, and just when I discovered I was four months pregnant, Lance got orders to Okinawa. It would seem our relationship was over…but God had other plans for us.

As Lance moved from duty station to duty station, another Marine moved along with him. This Marine was a strong Christian who began witnessing to my husband. His love for God started a chain of events that changed our lives forever.

I was the one who'd been baptized and confirmed. I was the one who attended church on all the special occasions growing up, not my husband. So when he tried to share his newfound faith with me, I proclaimed he was a Jesus freak. Who did he think he was, telling me about Jesus? We had a huge fight when Lance told me I was going to hell. Then he went to Okinawa, and I moved in with his family.

In Okinawa, who should show up as Lance's roommate but the Marine who had been witnessing to him. Slowly he nurtured Lance's faith, overcoming the damage I had done. In the meantime God began to slowly work on my heart. Living with my in-laws was difficult for all of us. I was crammed into Lance's old room, which had been promised to his little sister, and she, being the adolescent she was, had a tough time accepting me. We didn't like each other at all. I couldn't work because I was a Canadian living in America without my Social Security number yet. And I was pregnant. I couldn't go home and live with my family because we wanted the baby to be born in America.

As the months crawled by, Lance attended the Overseas Christian Serviceman's Center where his new faith was fed and exercised, and he became strong and firmly rooted. His letters home became filled with love and patience, not judging or blaming. We started to fall in love all over again. I wanted to know why and how this change had come to him.

In the meantime my doctor was concerned about my health: physical, mental, and emotional. As my due date drew close, she wrote, via the Red Cross, requesting emergency leave for Lance, so I wouldn't be alone for the delivery. Lance, via his new faith, firmly believed he would be granted emergency leave and he would be there. But the Marine Corps had other ideas.

The first time the letter was received, the Marine Corps Command pulled my husband away from his duties, told him to pack up, he was heading for home. By the time they got to the airport, the final signature was all that was needed. That was when the Navy Commander quoted the infamous "laying of the keel" saying.

Lance Corporal Lane Baldwin with son, Josh—"This time, prayers were answered, and answered swiftly. In a matter of hours, miraculously some would say, Lance was on a plane coming home to us."

Lance headed back to his barracks, disappointed, but not dejected. As he walked across the large parade field he heard, in his spirit, God confirm that he would indeed be home for our child's birth.

Back in Washington state I developed toxemia and had to go on partial bed rest. The doctor issued another Red Cross alert, requesting Lance be sent home immediately, and this time, I too prayed. Lance assured me it didn't matter what these men said to him because God had said, "Yes."

This time, prayers were answered and answered swiftly. In a matter of hours, miraculously some would say, Lance was on a plane coming home to us.

The rest of the story is just as inspiring. Our new faith was tested and our trust in the Lord was stretched when our son was two weeks late. Lance had only two weeks of leave. He asked for an extension, which is hardly ever granted, but this time it was. The night before Lance was to head back to Okinawa, our son, Joshua, was born. Lance spent all night with him and flew out at 10:00 AM the next day.

God's plan is flawless: He sent a strong believer into Lance's life at exactly the right moment—a pivotal tool in the building of our new life. From that point forward He continued to open doors and answered prayers that to this day amaze us. Sometimes God says yes, and sometimes He says no. But always He is in control, and that is a lesson we continue to learn daily—years after the answered military prayer.

❧ ❧ ❧

⌁ *The World's Greatest Fighter Pilot* ⌁

Ellie Kay, Palmdale, California

How do you react when you're on drugs?"

The question from the nurse surprised me as I stuttered, "Uh, well...you see I don't take drugs, so I don't know how I react."

"Well, your chart says you had ear surgery 15 years ago on your other ear; how did you do on anesthesia back then?" she asked, smiling.

"I remember waking up, too early, on the table in surgery as they were finishing the procedure. It was a horrifying experience and not one I'd care to repeat." I noted her surprise.

"Well, that won't happen here!" she announced firmly.

Hours later, in pre-op, I looked around the room at the other patients and said a quick prayer for them. Some were there for far more serious surgeries than mine. I remembered the cliché: "Minor surgery is when it's happening to someone else." My stapedotomy was a relatively new procedure that *repaired* rather than *replaced* the stapes bone in my inner ear. I already had a prosthetic stapes in my other ear when they did another procedure that was called a stapedectomy.

I was thankful that Dr. Horn, the surgeon, was the same doctor who pioneered this new procedure, and he had performed 2000 of these delicate surgeries. Furthermore, our insurance covered the $10,000 bill. Sure, I had to travel to a city four hours away from home and it took eight *years* of waiting to be in the right place at the right time. But I was thankful to have the chance to restore even part of my hearing in my deaf left ear. I was tired of reading lips and putting conversations together contextually. Most people didn't know the extent of my hearing loss because I didn't announce it often.

They just thought I was kind of ditzy—which would be true more often than not.

As I waited for my anesthesiologist, I thought about Bob waiting for me in the surgery waiting room. My thoughts grew melancholy as I recalled the news we received earlier in the month—Bob had been passed over for full colonel. He didn't seem upset that an upwardly progressive pattern as an Air Force officer was abruptly halted for him. When the news was released, he just said, "I gave this promotion to the Lord a long time ago, Ellie. If my Air Force career is winding down, then God has something much better planned for our family."

Even though he had a great attitude, I wondered what the news meant to him—as a man. Ever since the movie *Top Gun* came out, I'd joked that he was the "World's Greatest Fighter Pilot." Since we'd received that career blow, I'd tried to reinforce him verbally. Recalling this shared disappointment summoned unbidden tears.

My thoughts were interrupted by the anesthesiologist, "Well, Ellie, this stuff will work in about 15 seconds. Hey, I see that you guys live in Alamogordo."

I wiped my eyes as he continued, "My son and I were out at the White Sands and saw the Stealth flying around out there."

"Yes," I replied while waiting for the medication to take effect. "My husband flies the Stealth." By now I was starting to feel a little groggy, but continued, "If you and your son want to come and see it some time, just give us a call. My medical chart has our unlisted phone number on it. Just remind me that you were my anesthesiologist."

"But," the doctor said, "but…you probably won't *remember* this conversation!"

"Then why don't you go into the waiting room and talk to my husband, Bob." The drugs were definitely doing their job as I grew less inhibited. "Darlin', you just tell him about this conversation and you'll be covered."

"There's about 50 people out there in the waiting room—which one is your husband?" he quickly asked as I began to fade.

I smiled happily, "Why, just go ask for the 'World's Greatest Fighter Pilot.'"

So he did.

They wheeled me into the operating room, and I crawled from the gurney to the table and lay down. That's the last thing I remember. The forty-five minute procedure went well, and the doctor was pleased.

In the recovery room I remember coming in and out of consciousness muttering strange things, like…"I'm an arthur."

A faint voice answered me, "You are? You're an author? What do you write?"

I heard myself saying, "I write booksh like the best-shelling, *Shop, Shave, and Share*. I just finished a new one, *How to Shave Money Every Day*…about shaving money."

A while later I heard them say, "Well, it looks like our dream author is waking up."

I opened my eyes to see a nurse standing over me, "Do you have anyone waiting for you in the waiting room?" she asked.

"Yes" I said weakly as I tried to focus on her face, "Yes, my husband is out there."

The nurse gently asked, "Which one is he?"

I smiled dreamily and repeated my earlier instructions, "Just go ask for the 'World's Greatest Fighter Pilot.'"

So she did.

You might think that my "Beloved" Bob was embarrassed by medical professionals calling out in the waiting-room area, "Excuse me, is the 'World's Greatest Fighter Pilot' here?" But he's not. Amazingly, he loves me anyway.

He just shrugged his shoulders, stood up in the waiting area, and said, "Uh, that would be me—she must be awake now."

We went into the hospital with the purpose of having my hearing restored. But God never wastes an opportunity—His plans always serve more purposes than just one. We left with more than just restored hearing. You see, in that waiting room, my beloved *heard* that despite career setbacks and his uncertain professional future—his wife, both consciously and unconsciously, valued him greatly. His prayers had been answered that day by a messenger nurse.

Years of mutual affirmation and support from my guy make me want to let Bob know that I still think he's the World's Greatest Fighter Pilot.

So I did.

8

Life Changes

FREQUENT LIFE CHANGES ARE part of military life. The old joke is when the military says, "Jump," the correct response is, "How high?" But when told to "pack and move," that's no joke. You can make your requests, but it is the military's decision where you are placed, and you can either become miserable or heed Abram's example. This goes for changes not only in housing and location, but changes in rank as well.

Thanks be to God, believers have a Higher Authority who listens to our grievances, who moves on our behalf, and sometimes even directs the military in what to do. When God says, "Go," believers need only answer, "Wherever You say, Lord," even when He uses the armed services to get us to our destination. God was moving people around for His glory long before the military. And no matter what those in authority say, when we trust God, He will get us where we need to be.

❧❧❧

The LORD had said to Abram, "Leave your country,
your people and your father's household and go to the land
I will show you.". . . So Abram left.

GENESIS: 12:1,4

⌐ *God Is Our Landlord* ∽

TOINETTE F. WELCH, HUNTSVILLE, ALABAMA

WHEN U.S. SOUTHERN COMMAND moved from Panama to Miami in the summer of 1997, it provoked fear and apprehension for many military families. It wasn't simply because Miami carried a rougher reputation (perhaps unjustly) than, say, Kansas City or Seattle. It was that, plus the fact there was no military post there, just a new building for the U.S. SouthCom Headquarters. No post meant no housing, no chapel, no Protestant Women of the Chapel (PWOC), no central place to congregate, and no support system. Miami is a big place to be "on your own."

Pam, a friend from the Ft. Clayton (Panama) PWOC, and I knew we needed to pray about this. One night after a PWOC program, we prayed together before getting into our cars. We prayed we would find houses to rent close enough to each other so our sons could attend the ninth grade together, be in the same scout troop, and Pam and I would have a friend close by.

We arranged to spend a week in the Miami area looking for houses to rent. Each family had different requirements for a home, but we both decided Broward County might offer a quieter environment with good schools. Before my husband, John, and I met with our realtor, we drove randomly through several neighborhoods "window shopping." We saw a tiny "for rent" sign sitting in a window and pulled into the driveway to peek inside.

Within minutes, a realtor's car pulled up behind ours and much to our surprise, out stepped our friends, Pam and Jeff! What a "coincidence" that out of the hundreds of houses for rent their realtor could have taken them to, we both would be at the exact same house at exactly the same time. As we walked through the house, we exchanged hotel information so we could call each other about our house-hunting results. As it turned out, the house we were all looking at had already been rented, so we went our separate ways.

That night or the next, Pam called to tell me she and Jeff had found a house and were off to the Florida Keys for some R&R before returning to Panama to pack up. I tucked her new address into my wallet but had no good news of my own to give her. John and I continued to house hunt through the week, finally coming to one last rental to check out. If this one didn't work out, we'd have to plug a new set of parameters into the realtor's computer and start all over.

The house was boxy and contemporary, and not like anything we'd normally choose, but it felt "right" when I walked into it. Hearing there was a restriction against pets, and we had a puppy, I prayed a quick prayer to God: "Lord, if this house is for us, I know You will find a way to work this out."

A phone call later, the owner relented with a pet deposit written into the contract.

With all the papers signed, I walked outside to the car to get Pam's address and our map. I wanted to find out how far away she was and how I would get to her house. I stared at the address in amazement. I simply could not believe my eyes. Her house was right next door. I can still hear John saying, "Do you think God is chuckling right now?"

God is not only *able* to provide for our wishes and needs; He is *willing* to do just that. I am still constantly amazed that the God of the universe would involve Himself with the small matters in the life of each individual, but that is who He is: Sovereign God of all time and space, and yet "Abba," providing abundantly for His children.

"Thank You, Lord."

↭ *Divine Assignment* ↝

WENDY FIL, HUNTSVILLE, ALABAMA

FOR TWENTY-EIGHT YEARS, God has blessed my husband, Joe, in his military career. We have had our share of roadblocks along the way, all of which have been opportunities for us to remember to focus on the Giver and not the gifts. These have been times for us to build "spiritual muscle" by paying attention to His Word. There have been countless times for us to seek His guidance through prayer.

I remember when my husband was a major, preparing to graduate from the Command and General Staff College in Kansas. He wanted to be assigned as a staff officer in a battalion, in hopes that one day he might qualify for a command. This was the path that career Army officers needed to take, and it was the path that we were prepared for.

"Lord, please position me in this type of job. Please guide me with Your hand," Joe prayed throughout his year of school, which finally came to an end. Graduation day was here, and we were going to see what was on the horizon. It was an exciting time. We waited in anticipation for the assignments officer in Washington, D.C., to call and tell us the next step of our military journey.

The assignments officer finally called and gave him the news—we were off to Germany, where Joe would be assigned as the operations officer. Terrific! Praise God! He had answered our prayers. We excitedly began to make our plans and ship our household goods. Our entire house of furniture and hundreds of boxes holding our memories and possessions were crated up and on their way across the Atlantic.

Before flying to Germany, we visited his parents in California, having one more chance to visit family before we moved halfway around the world. While there, we received a call from his branch headquarters that would turn our lives upside down.

"The Chief of Staff of the Army needs a travel officer, Major, and the job is yours if you want it." The voice boomed from the other end of the receiver.

"Thanks, let me think about it…" was all Joe could reply. My husband was humbled and grateful to have been selected. Still, deep in his heart, he longed for the opportunity to command a battalion. Left with the decision, we did the only thing we knew to do. We turned to the Father in prayer, asking for His guidance, even His divine intervention. We prayed knowing He had a purpose for us and a place He wanted us to be. We wanted to be in the center of God's will, wherever it might take us. We just didn't know which path to take. The next morning, the phone rang again.

"Major, we've decided to give the job to another person. If you want the opportunity to command, you need to serve as a staff officer in a battalion now."

We knew God had answered our prayers and directed our path. He was faithful in all things, from the smallest detail to the greatest.

My husband eventually did command a battalion, and we have learned through the years, whether in prosperity or testing, to seek God's guidance through prayer. We know that all the details of our lives have been directed, just as God has orchestrated believers from the foundation of the world. He knew every problem and provided every solution before we came into existence. What great comfort that brings! In His grace, God provided prayer—a way for us to express our faith in Him, that His presence and love might be a reality in our lives. For He has always known the desires of our hearts.

∿ A U-Turn from Panama ∿

CANDY ZARCONE, THERESA, NEW YORK

Honey, I'm pregnant!" Oh what joy and excitement—our first baby!

Then several months into my pregnancy, my husband announced, "I've received orders from the Army to go to Panama." Before marriage, I had helped with missions work in Mexico, so I excitedly exclaimed, "This is great. The Army is paying our way to help with missions in Panama, and I already know the language."

"That's not all," my husband continued. "I have three months of school in Virginia before we go to Panama, so we've got time to prepare."

Moving details began, and before we knew it, I was in the hospital having the baby just as the movers were packing our household goods to be shipped to Panama.

Having a C-section warranted a four-day hospital stay, and our associate pastor and his wife offered to let us stay with them until we could be on our way to Virginia. As I rested after leaving the hospital, my husband called his counselor at the Department of the Army to check in.

"What?" I heard him stammer. "Yes, I understand. Well, let me ask her…" I overheard my husband saying, as a lump settled in my stomach.

"Honey, they've decided not to send us to Panama after my training in Virginia. How about Fort Drum, New York?"

"Do we have a choice?" I replied, knowing full well we did not.

The adjustments of being first-time parents consumed those three months of training in Virginia. Before we knew it, the time had flown by, and we were attending our last church service before our move to New York.

"Tony and Candy, would you come forward and let us pray for you before you leave?"

In prayer, our pastor lifted up all our concerns about a new home, new church, and new friends.

After the service an evangelist approached my husband, "I haven't seen you here before, because I have been traveling and ministering, but I know of a great church up in the Fort Drum area. Let me give you the address and the pastor's information."

After arriving in New York, we called the church and made plans to attend. The small congregation was warm and friendly. After the service, the pastor and his wife invited us over for lunch. We shared our recent life events, how we had been preparing for our move to Panama, but at the last minute were surprised to receive the new orders that had brought us here. We talked about our experience in church and told them we enjoyed serving and offered to help however needed.

"We've been praying for you!" they said almost in tandem. "For three months we've been praying for the Lord to send a couple who would help us in ministry."

Tony and I looked at each other and smiled. It had taken us three months to get there, with a few turns along the way, but it was comforting to know that we had become the answer to their fervent prayers for help. In that moment, everything made perfect sense.

Though the Army may think they tell us where to go, it is God who ultimately directs our steps.

⌣ *Military Brat* ↬

Maryanne Coronna, St. Paul, Minnesota

My son, Aaron, accepted Jesus into his heart when he was only three years old. He would later tell me he hadn't remembered doing this, which was why, at thirteen, he again committed his life to Christ during a summer basketball camp. The pride and joy he had always brought to my life and our shared love for the Lord provided the glue that kept our relationship close—even during those teen years.

Then 9/11 happened, and he did something that would send our relationship, and my faith in God, into a tailspin. He committed his life to the United States Marine Corps.

It was Aaron who had called us from his college apartment, telling us to turn the TV on the morning the World Trade Towers were attacked. My husband and I, like the rest the nation, sat glued to the screen as the horrific events unfolded before our eyes. We witnessed the black billows of smoke against a blue sky in a city landscape home to more than eight million Americans. As a family, we had, two weeks prior, visited New York City to celebrate our daughter's sixteenth birthday.

The attack reminded me of the Japanese attack on Pearl Harbor, which landed my father and my husband's father in the Pacific Theater during World War II. On 9/11 we mourned for our country. But Aaron, whose best friend had been his Grandpa Coronna, a veteran firefighter and a veteran of war, took the attack personally.

In the ensuing months, I watched him grow into a serious student of war. He treated the process of applying to the Officer Candidate School more seriously than he had his college admissions. I believed he was going through a phase that would pass, like when he switched majors from pre-dentistry to business and political science.

He sent for academic and medical records, took the required physical, and asked friends and relatives with military backgrounds to write letters of recommendation. So I got busy too. Prayer took a front seat to everything else. I was convinced this was *not* the will of God. I asked the Lord to reverse his direction and to show Aaron that this "phase," while noble, was just that—a phase—and he needed to get on with his life.

But in the summer of 2002, he was accepted into the Officer Candidate School program, and my hope faded. I questioned God's love and sovereignty. I reminded the Lord I was, after all, the child's earthly parent who knew what was best for her son. I reminded the Lord the world was spinning out of control, and He needed to step up and be God. Daily I reminded Him it was His responsibility to take revenge against the evil, in all its terrorist forms, and leave my son out of this. I reminded God I did not bring this boy into the world to fight wars, much less to die in one.

Whenever a thought came into my head about the possibility this was, perhaps, God's design for Aaron's life, I argued against it, stated my rights before the Almighty, stomped my foot, and slammed the door to my heart. "Not my son!" I cried. "Not my only son!"

After his first six-week training in Quantico, Virginia, Aaron came home to begin his junior year of college. I was in graduate school at the time, and it wasn't uncommon for us to stay up late together studying. One night as I sat at my desk typing at the computer, we began to argue, as we often did, about the war and his military aspirations.

"Mom!" he yelled. "You're the one who's taught me to follow my conscience! You're the person who's told me since I was a little boy, 'Aaron, don't listen to the crowd! Listen to God!'" He shifted his body to the edge of his chair and leaned into the space between us.

"You've told me," he continued, pointing his index finger and suddenly becoming me, "Aaron, I'm going to die. You're going to die. We are all going to die. And when we do, we will stand face-to-face before Almighty God, and at that moment, we will have to account for our lives."

He settled back into the overstuffed chair, as if resting into a peaceful assurance—a place my stubborn heart would not enter, much less share with him. "Well, Mom," his eyes pleading with me to follow his logic, "if I die at age 23, doing what I know God asked me to do, dying because He used me in something bigger than myself, dying to defend our freedom and liberty, then you should be happy."

It was late; I was tired of fighting. I did not resist. Instead, I surrendered into the ever-beckoning arms of resentment. My darkest days would follow. Although I did not grow up as a "military brat," I had become a real one by my actions. But God was patient with me and walked with me, even as I stepped further and further into fear and rebelliousness—as a spoiled brat always does.

On the outside, I was as supportive as I could pretend to be; on the inside, I was wrestling with God on a daily basis. My prayer life seemed dead. And while I didn't want Aaron to fail, I knew with one more grueling six-week training course coming up that summer, there was still a glimmer of hope God would show up and weed him out.

Aaron again left at the end of May. In the meantime, we bought plane tickets and made hotel reservations, fully expecting him to graduate on July 3. Graduation from OCS would mean that he had passed every physical, mental, and academic challenge required for his commissioning.

Then, on a late-June afternoon, the phone rang. It was Aaron. His voice was shaky, as if trying to contain some great force of despair. He asked me to pray for him. "I don't think I'm going to make it, Mom," he said. My heart soared, then sank. This was the moment I'd waited for; but, at the same time, I realized my son was asking me for help. I'd been living a double life. Among friends and family members who supported the war in Iraq, I smiled bravely and agreed with them: "Yes, isn't it wonderful that Aaron wants to become a Marine." In my prayer closet, I demanded God intervene and return my son's heart to that of a civilian.

"Aaron," I said, "Remember Nehemiah 8:10: 'The joy of the LORD is your strength.'"

"Wait," he said, making a mental note of it. "Tell me the verse again."

I felt like a hypocrite. But in that moment, a peace came rushing over me. I can only describe what I felt as an overwhelming sense of letting go. As if releasing my grip from a rough and sweat-stained rope. The tug-o-war was over. I surrendered to God in that moment as best I could.

"Well, Aaron," I assured him, "Dad and I will pray for you. You've come so far and worked so hard. Just keep your eyes on Jesus." Aaron had two weeks to go, and they would prove to be the most difficult, most challenging of all his training. I hung up the phone that afternoon, telling the Lord in earnest, "Thy will be done." And I prayed for Aaron as he had asked me to.

Something within my heart began to soften. As I heard my son's voice in my head saying, "I don't think I'm going to make it, Mom," I heard the voice of the Father, reminding me of His love for Jesus, who He allowed to die on the cross for my sake. "This is my Son, whom I love; with him I am well pleased" (Matthew 17:5).

I slowly gave every rebellious thought and fear over to Christ. As I prayed for Aaron, I told the Lord I would accept whatever happened as His good and perfect will for his life. The Lord gave me 1 John 4:9, "This is how God showed his love among us: He sent his one and only Son into the world that we might live through him."

God was faithful—He changed my heart and gave Aaron the strength he needed to continue. And on June 12, 2004, he was commissioned to the rank of second lieutenant. Aaron is now serving in Okinawa, Japan.

Military "Brat" Maryanne Coronna with son, Second Lieutenant Aaron Coronna, and husband, Mark—"Well, Mom, if I die at age 23, doing what I know God asked me to do, dying because He used me in something bigger than myself, dying to defend our freedom and liberty, then you should be happy."

God answered my prayers in a way I had never expected. In saying no to me, His sovereign plan was carried out exactly as He wished.

Recently, a woman stopped me in a parking lot. Pointing to the decal on my car that reads "Proud parent of a U.S. Marine," she commented on how she too was proud of our troops. I nodded politely and said, "I'm going to redesign that decal and replace the word "proud" with "humbled" because it's not pride that I feel at all, but humility. That my son should willingly lay down his life—it humbles me every day."

∽: *Belief, Doubt, Belief* :∽

TERESA PUCKETT, GROVETOWN, GEORGIA

ON JANUARY 21, 1999, a month-and-a-half before my husband, John, turned 32, he followed God's leading and enlisted in the U.S. Army. Since obtaining his bachelors degree prior to enlistment, he was told he would be able to apply for Officer Candidate School (OCS) once he finished basic training.

Upon completion of basic training, John was sent to the Defense Language Institute (DLI) in Monterey, California, to learn Arabic, where he was then told he could apply for OCS after he completed his training there. In May 2000, the information changed. He was told he would have to finish all of his training and spend a full year at his first permanent station before he could apply. The extent of his training at DLI, and any additional training at Goodfellow Air Force Base in Texas, would take four years. He would be nearly thirty-five years old before being allowed to apply for Officer Candidate School, and the Army informed him they would not accept his application at that point because of his age.

John's commanding officer believed in him and didn't want him to be held back on a technicality, so he was allowed to apply to the Navy OCS. He quickly submitted his Navy packet before he left for Texas at the beginning of August. He was told the application process would take six weeks.

Time wore on, and during this period, I had been cofacilitating the *Experiencing God* Bible study at the Protestant Woman of the Chapel in Monterey, where God was using our circumstances to help me fully experience Him.

Fifteen weeks after submitting his OCS packet to the Navy, John told me he had received an e-mail from his Navy OCS recruiter earlier that afternoon, and the answer was no.

"No?" I gripped the phone tightly, numb for a minute, not knowing how to respond. I thought God had clearly set our path. How could we have been so wrong? John tried to console me, but I really needed time to discuss this with God.

As I struggled through this, a dear friend and my sister both spoke the same thing to me: "If God promised something to you, it isn't over yet." I was encouraged by their words because my husband and I really felt as though God had indeed promised this to us, but I couldn't see beyond my doubt.

My faith told me that God doesn't change His mind. Genesis 22, where God told Abraham to sacrifice his son Isaac kept playing through my mind. Abraham knew God had told him to sacrifice his son, but at the last moment, God stopped him. But what did this have to do with my family and John's not going to Navy OCS? Yes, it would be a sacrifice to have John away from our family for training and six-month deployments each year, but that was nothing in comparison to the magnitude of sacrifice Abraham was asked to make.

I shared my thoughts with my sister, and she pointed me to the beginning of the story, where God promised Abraham that He would make a great nation through Isaac. The sacrifice was the middle of the greater story and, ultimately, God fulfilled His promise through Isaac.

Was this the middle of my family's story? Two days later, finally at peace with the decision, I reminded myself that God's ways are unique and different from mine. In prayer I told the Lord I trusted Him and knew that His path was best, even if I never gained full understanding of our situation. I resolved that whatever the outcome, I would rejoice in His path set before us.

Preparing for Bible study, I reviewed the previous lessons and what God desired in response to each lesson. I had known the truth outlined in the lessons for years, but in the midst of my crisis of belief, I found it easy to forget. Yes, God was faithful to Abraham, but Abraham *knew* he had heard God. Could I say that? As I searched my heart and went back over the promises God had given me during that time, I was sure I had.

"See, I am doing a new thing! Now it springs up; do you not perceive it? I am making a way in the desert and streams in the wasteland" (Isaiah 43:19). When He gave me this particular promise, I was so focused on the Navy that I didn't take into account that He could be doing a new thing that I did not perceive. The fact is, God was doing "a new thing" in our family's life.

When this realization hit me, I was immediately filled with such excitement to see the rest of God's promise that I no longer cared which direction it took. Previously I had been too focused on what I thought God's plan was, and I failed to seek His perspective. "'For I know the plans I have for you,' declares the LORD, 'plans to prosper you and not to harm you, plans to give you hope and a future. Then you will call upon me and come and pray to me, and I will listen to you. You will seek me and find me when you seek me with all your heart'" (Jeremiah 29:11-13).

Nearly five years have passed since receiving that phone call in Monterey, California. Has God's entire plan been revealed to us yet? No, but He has consistently provided enough of His promise for us to follow in His path.

While still enlisted and proudly serving as an Arabic linguist in the Army, God has allowed John the opportunity to attend seminary and work toward his Master of Divinity degree. We're pretty certain had John been accepted into the Navy OCS, this wouldn't have been a path he could have taken. He still has two-thirds of his credit hours yet to complete, and God has not shown us exactly how He desires this degree to be used, but John and I continue to serve Him where He has placed us.

As for me, God used that time of belief and doubt to grow my faith. And as a result, I will be equipped to better serve Him as I continue to serve the ladies God has placed in ministry around me. May it be said of me, "Yet [she] did not waver through unbelief regarding the promise of God, but was strengthened in faith and gave glory to God, being fully persuaded that God had power to do what he had promised" (Romans 4:20-21).

God continues to answer the prayers of our hearts as John and I experience the awesome way He has of orchestrating life when we remove all doubt and allow Him to be in control.

◡: My Own Pilgrim's Progress :◡

SERGEANT GLEN W. HAMBRICK, FORT BELVOIR, VIRGINIA

IN JULY OF 2001, I arrived at the Primary Leadership Development Course (PLDC) at Fort Campbell, Kentucky. PLDC is required for any specialist to be promoted to sergeant. At the time my family and I really needed the pay raise. If I didn't pass PLDC, I wouldn't be promoted, and without the promotion, we couldn't replace our only car, which had died part way through my course. My wife and two daughters would suffer the consequences of my failure. The pressure to pass weighed on me like a 100-pound rucksack.

The hardest part of the course was map reading and land navigation. In the classroom we learned how to read a topographical map and use a compass and a protractor to plot coordinates. This wasn't so hard, but in the field it was far more difficult as we tried to use all the techniques we learned to find points in a designated area. Knowing that the majority of the people who didn't pass PLDC failed during land navigation added greatly to the pressure I was under. If I failed, I would have to wait six months before I could try again.

Finally the day came to apply our classroom skills to real life on the land navigation course. The morning started off comfortable, but it was getting hotter by the minute. The training area known as the Back 40 was one of the worst training environments imaginable. At this time of the year, it was all very green and thick. It was wild and oppressive and composed of various types of terrain, a lot of gnarled trees, and many thorn bushes.

The moment of truth arrived. Our instructor assigned four grid coordinates for each soldier to plot on a map. To pass land navigation, we were required to locate three of them within three hours; finding all four was a sign of a consummate soldier. Our mission was to locate the large wooden poles, which marked the points. Each was approximately six feet high with a green plastic silhouette of a soldier with a number on it.

The truck stopped. I was ready. I had everything I needed, including my prescription sunglasses, which became a symbol of comfort and confidence for me later. I was like the pilgrim Christian walking to the Celestial City—or so I hoped.

During this practice session, two things went wrong. First, I misjudged the distances between points. As a result, I became lost and wandered aimlessly through the woods. I also lost the card on which I had to write the grid points and numbers from the silhouettes. This was an automatic no-go: failure.

The test day started out better. I found my first two points with ease. The second point wasn't too far from my end point. I could have found my end point, checked in, and received a GO from my instructor. But I wanted to find the third point so I could get four of four.

Big mistake. While trying to find the third point, I got lost. I encountered more thorn bushes, receiving deep red scratches all over my legs, which reflected how I felt in my heart—defeated and miserable, just like Christian in *Pilgrim's Progress,* who went off the designated path. Every time a branch broke under my foot or I felt a thorn scratch my leg, my mind would race. Crack! *You've failed land navigation—you're not going to be promoted.* Snap! *No new car for you.* Crunch! *You might as well give up now.*

As I searched for the last point, I suddenly realized my compass was gone. I was stranded in the woods. Finally I found another soldier and followed him, not caring if he knew where he was going. It was the blind leading the blind. We ended up on a long dirt road out in the middle of nowhere. We were so exhausted, we could go no farther, so we sat on the roadside. I was sweaty, smelly, tired, and dehydrated. Eventually we got up, walked to the main road, and collapsed.

An instructor found us along the road and returned us to the start site, where we were transported back to school. Riding the bus was a relief. I was free, delivered from that place of thorns and pain. But in the back of my mind was a realization I would be going back there...the next day.

After the test, we were released to spend time with our families. I desperately wanted to talk to my wife. I wanted to hold her, to cry in her arms, to be encouraged by her, to rally the strength to try again. But I didn't have her there to console me; she was visiting my parents in New Mexico.

Instead I called my best friend, Doug Chace, who turned out to be a real answer to prayer. He took me to his house, and I called my wife. The second I heard her voice I crashed to rock bottom. All the strength I had harnessed in order to keep it together melted away. I was so discouraged, I cried like a baby. All that pressure to pass the course, to provide for my family, to replace my car, was weighing me down, and I broke. I felt I had failed my family and my God. All my wife could do was comfort me over the phone and pray for me. She told my mom, who in turn called her church. Everyone who knew me, knew my mother, and some who didn't know me from Adam, lifted up prayers to God to help me.

After I talked to my wife, Doug could tell I was very depressed and decided to give me some pointers. He's a helicopter pilot who knows land navigation very well. He also gave me his Officer Candidacy coin for good luck and bought me an expensive compass to replace the one I lost. That unselfish act caught me off guard; it was like ointment for my soul.

The day of the re-test arrived. I awoke feeling refreshed and confident, although no one in my class thought I would pass. Our group was dropped off at the designated point, where we plotted the points on our map and prepared to leave. Reaching into my pocket, I felt Doug's coin and was reminded of God's provision. Whispering a simple prayer for help and guidance, I sought to correct my course and get back on the path to Celestial City.

I found the first point without any difficulty. However, I ran into a problem with my second point. I came upon a clearing where I thought the point would be, but it wasn't there. I didn't panic; I took a deep breath, looked at the map, and realized the point was beside a depression—a slightly sunken area near the tree line. I located the depression and found my second point!

Suddenly I realized I was running out of time. I had to find my finish point, and I had to do it quickly! I became lost again—but not hopelessly. I found the road that intersected the path to my finish point. I did some quick figuring and started walking fast! I located my goal, noted my finish point, and raced to the check-in site. I gave my card to the group leader, who checked my points and told me to get back on the bus going back to school. I had passed.

I had relied on God to guide me. He heard my prayers and the prayers of those I love. Finally, I could let go of the pressure to pass the course—tossing that 100-pound rucksack to the ground. I passed land navigation. I would be promoted, and I could buy our family a new car. I hadn't let my wife and girls down after all.

News of our successes or failures had preceded us to the barracks. I walked in and my classmates cheered. I went to my bunk and people started coming to me saying, "Gosh, Hambrick, no one thought you would make it. Good job!" Outwardly, I thanked them, but to myself I thanked God for helping me with my own pilgrim's progress. I know He answered my prayers that day, and it forever changed the course of my life.

Author Bios

Jean Adams has been married 18 years to her high school sweetheart, SFC Thomas Adams, U.S. Army. She is mother to three beautiful children. Jean is passionate about the Lord and women's ministry with a 10-year involvement with Protestant Women of the Chapel. She also speaks at retreats and special events. Contact: gvmejesus@yahoo.com

Charlotte Adelsperger has authored three books and written for more than 100 publications, including, *Focus on the Family, Clubhouse,* and *Woman's World.* She is a popular speaker who lives in a suburb of Kansas City. Contact: author04@aol.com

Nancy C. Anderson (www.NancyCAnderson.com) is the author of *Avoiding the Greener Grass Syndrome: How to Grow Affair-Proof Hedges Around Your Marriage.* She is also a popular speaker at women's and couples' events. Nancy lives in Southern California with her husband of 26 years and their son. Contact: NancyCAnderson@msn.com

Linda Mae Baldwin lives with her husband, Lance, in the Pacific Northwest. Current writing includes an online column at dancingword.net and an article in the June 2005 edition of *Romantic Homes* magazine. For more information, visit her website at www.lindamaebaldwin.com.

Rachel I. Blevins grew up in a missionary home in the Cayman Islands. She homeschooled three sons, worked in hospice care, and has mentored young mothers. She is married to Pastor Joe and delights in granddaughters Montana and Mycah.

C. Hope Clark is a retired federal manager and full-time freelance writer living in South Carolina. She founded FundsforWriters.com, a resource for career writers that has won a *Writer's Digest* award for five straight years. She authored *The Shy Writer*. Website: www.fundsforwriters.com

Maryanne Coronna holds an M.F.A. in creative writing from Hamline University in St. Paul, Minnesota, where she lives with her husband, Mark, and two-year-old golden retriever, Milo. She is a freelance writer and editor and teaches writing at Bethel University.

Ginger Cox, raised in a military family, credits her parents and the Protestant chapels across the country for her formal Christian education, providing a strong foundation for her own values and beliefs. For this, she is eternally grateful. Website: www.GingerCox.com

Rona Cunningham is a thirty-one-year-old wife, mother, daughter, sister, and friend. Husband Dwayne of fourteen years, and Lauren 11, Brittney 10, and Wayne 6, are her inspiration. She is a Christian by God's grace, not of works, praise God for the blood! Ronabelle@ hotmail.com

G. E. Dabbs is Senior Chaplain Assistant with the 110th Chaplain Detachment in Birmingham, Alabama. He's published *Lucy's Treasure* and *For the Love of Alice*. Married to Patty, they share six children: Aaron, Joshua, Tim, Amanda, Carmen, and Edward. Contact: dabbsge@juno.com

Jennifer Devlin is an Army wife and women's ministry leader with a vibrant speaking, writing, and teaching ministry. She lives with her amazing husband and son in North Alabama. Please visit her website www.ministryforlife.com or email her at jennifer@ministryforlife.com

Rev. Patricia A. Duncan, founder of Shekanah Glory Outreach World-wide, Lecturer and Associate Overseas Director of World Missions Ministries Bible College, has preached the gospel all over the world including India, Africa, and Central and South America to the glory of God. Contact: revduncan@aol.com

Eva Marie Everson has made an impact in Christian publishing in a matter of a few years, by crossing genres and rarely being predictable. Since 1999 she has written, compiled, and edited books of both fiction and nonfiction, including *The Potluck Club* and *Sex, Lies, and the Media.* Website: www.evamarieeverson.com

Susan Farr Fahncke is the author of *Angel's Legacy* and coauthor and contributor of numerous other books. Susan runs Angels2TheHeart, a foundation sending care packages and cards to critically ill people. She lives in Utah and teaches online writing workshops. Visit her website at www.2TheHeart.com. Email her at Editor@2TheHeart.com

Carleta Goodwin Fernandes lives in Amarillo, Texas, with husband, Rick. Retired after 20 years in law enforcement, she spends time reading about writing, talking about writing, and occasionally writing. Many of her stories are drawn from her life in police work and growing up Texan. Contact: carleta@cox.net

Command Sergeants Major Mark Gerecht has 24 years of service in the U.S. Army. His family consists of Patricia, his lovely wife of 23 years, and their daughter, Shania. He is a published author of five books and two CDs on leadership and other military-related subjects. Contact: mpsg1963@aol.com

Tricia Goyer is an author of five books and nationally known speaker. She lives with her family in Montana. Tricia interviewed over fifty WWII veterans for her novels *From Dust and Ashes* and *Night Song.* Tricia can be reached at tricia@thegoyers.com or www.triciagoyer.com

Caron Guillo lives in Texas with husband, Bob, and their three children. She devotes time to family, disciple-making, and writing. Caron loves partnering in service with Bob—now a full-time outreach minister—evangelistic praying, speaking to women's groups, traveling, and chocolate. Contact: Caron_guillo@hotmail.com

Pamela Hallal, mother of five, and her husband reside in Indianapolis, Indiana. They are long-time members of College Park Church. She currently does motivational and public speaking, teaching, operates a custom home decor business, and is a strong military advocate. Email her at p.hallal@integrity.com

Glen W. Hambrick lives in Fort Belvoir, Virginia. He is a Non-Commissioned Officer Human Resources Specialist who works for the Deputy Chief of Staff, G-8, in Washington, D.C. He and Lori, married 14 years, have two daughters: Nichole, 11, and Janae, 3.

Audrey Kletscher Helbling lives in Faribault, Minnesota, with husband, Randy, and children Amber, Miranda, and Caleb. Her work has appeared in *The Lutheran Digest, Minnesota Moments* magazine, poetry anthologies, greeting cards, and elsewhere. Faith, family, and her childhood home in southwestern Minnesota influence Audrey's writing.

Shawn M. Helgerson is a Staff Sergeant in the U.S. Air Force. He lives with his wife and five children in Washington state but calls New Hampshire home. He is also an apprentice in the Christian Writers Guild. His e-mail address is shawn.helgerson@att.net

Cynthia Hinkle is a freelance writer of devotions, stories, articles, and children's resources. She wrote the 2005 children's Christmas Arch®book *Star of Wonder.* Cynthia Hinkle's husband, research scientist Andrew Hinkle, and Staff Sgt. Forringer both worked for a corporation in Pittsburgh before the Hinkles relocated to Ohio.

Norman Holland enlisted in the Army in 1941. After 30 years of active duty with four overseas tours, he retired as a colonel in 1971. Married to Jeri for 59 years, they have a daughter Debra, son Jarrell, daughter-in-law Debbie, and grandson Jesse.

Pamela Johnson writes from her home in the Pacific Northwest. In 2004 she "adopted" two soldiers while they were stationed in Iraq. She wrote to them weekly until they completed their mission in Baghdad and safely returned stateside in January 2005.

Nelda Jones and husband, "Sonny," have five children and eight grandchildren. She does desktop publishing, and is media ministries director at her church. She has been published in many publications, including the "God's Abundance" series, and other books by Kathy Miller. Contact: NeldaFJones@aol.com

Ellie Kay is a media veteran, international speaker, and bestselling author of eight books, including the Gold Medallion book award finalist *Heroes at Home—Hope and Help for American Military Families*. Her life-changing military conferences are popular worldwide. For more info, go to www.elliekay.com or email her at ellie@elliekay.com

Brian and Ronie Kendig live near Fort Worth, Texas. Married for 15 years, they have four children and a golden retriever. Brian, a disabled veteran formerly with the U.S. Army's 10th Mountain Division, is a firearms instructor and history buff in his spare time. Contact: Kendig2@comcast.net. Ronie, an avid writer and member of the American Christian Fiction Writers, has had stories e-published and was spotlighted as the featured writer with a women's e-magazine. Visit Ronie at her website: www.roniekendig.com

Pat Knox is a CLASS graduate and the producer of a Christian talk radio program in St. Louis, Missouri. She and husband, Dan, have three adult children: Shannon, RN; Kelley, Creative Memories consultant/nanny; and Chris, U.S. Marines. Contact Pat at PKnoxMO@aol.com

Steven Manchester, the father of three beautiful children, is the published author of *The Rockin' Chair, The Unexpected Storm, A Father's Love,* and *Jacob Evans,* as well as several books under the pseudonym Steven Herberts. Three of his screenplays have been produced as films. Website: www.StevenManchester.com

Sandra McGarrity is a contributor to *God Allows U-Turns, A Woman's Journey and American Moments, God Answers Prayers,* and *God Answers Mom's Prayers.* Her work has also been published in various magazines. She is the author of two Christian fiction novels. Visit her website at www.heartwarmers4u.com/members?woody

De'on Miller studied creative writing as an undergraduate at Texas Tech University. She has previously published a short story, "Relativity: *Editha* Revisited" in *The Harbinger.* She resides in Lovington, New Mexico, with her husband and is currently at work on a collection of essays. Email her at deonmiller7@hotmail.com

Janet Lynn Mitchell is a wife, mother, author, and inspirational speaker. Her books include *A Special Kind of Love, For Those Who Love Children with Special Needs,* published by Broadman and Holman/Focus on the Family, and the *Hands-on Faith* series by Carson Dellosa, 2005. Website: www.JanetLynnMitchell.com; email her at JanetLM@prodigy.net

Gloria L. Penwell lives in Chattanooga, Tennessee, with husband, Dan. They have four children and seven grandchildren. Her most recent job was as liaison between Christian Book Distributors and the prisoners who purchased from them.

Major General James (Jim) H. Pillsbury commands the Army Aviation and Missile Command at Redstone Arsenal, Alabama. He holds degrees from Trinity University and Troy State University and has taught youth Sunday school classes in many of the eighteen locations he has lived in since joining the Army. Email him at Lifeliner6@aol.com

Teresa Puckett has been an Army wife for six years. She and husband, John, have been married over seventeen years and have four children, Stephen, 17; Carissa, 15; Benjamin, 11; and Jessica, 10. They are committed to serving God however He directs. Contact: tmpuckett@ hotmail.com

Kayleen J. Reusser is a freelance writer who specializes in travel, profiles, entertainment, and religious essays. She has published hundreds of articles in publications that include *Today's Christian Woman, Decision, Grit,* and *Fort Wayne News-Sentinel.* She is the editor of a newsletter for a jail chaplaincy. Contact: kjreusser@onlyinternet.net

Heather (Hansen) Ruppert was born in Nebraska and now resides with her husband and four children in Illinois. She is a homeschool mother as well as a child-care counselor at a child welfare agency. She enjoys reading, writing, and walking. Contact: hruppert@consolidated.net

"Father George" Rzasowski was born in Poland. He is a priest and a major in the U.S. Army. He enjoys the military life and riding his Harley Davidson motorcycle. He is loved by his congregation and community of faith.

Specialist Carlo Serrano has served five years in the Army as a Movement Control Specialist. He holds ministerial credentials with the Assemblies of God and leads the Singles/Young Adults ministry at First Assembly in Clarksville, TN.

Judy Spolarich, a school construction financial consultant to California public school districts, serves as an executive board member for a Christian high school in the Sacramento area. Her hobbies include banner making, traveling, sewing, and singing Italian opera. Judy has served as editor of several newsletters and publications.

Gloria Cassity Stargel, a writer for *Guideposts* and others, urgently asked, "Does God still heal today?" Result: Her award-winning book *The Healing, One Family's Victorious Struggle with Cancer.* Read portions at www.brightmorning.com. You can order online or call 1-800-888-9529 or write to Applied Images, 312 Bradford St NW, Gainesville, GA 30501.

Jerry H. Thomas was the first in the family (both sides) to get a college degree and become an Air Force pilot (flying "high brass" for three different tours). After forty years of wandering, he met Jesus Christ, and He has been his Comforter, Redeemer, and constant companion since 1976. Contact: jhjbthomas@earthlink.net

Christine Trollinger resides in Kansas City, Missouri, with her husband of forty-one years. She is the mother of three, grandmother of three, and great-grandmother of one great-grandchild named Grace. Christine is a published author of several short stories of inspiration.

Captain Mike Warren has served 10 years in the Army as both an enlisted soldier and an officer. He is currently serving as adjutant for the Oklahoma City Recruiting Battalion. He has been involved with discipleship ministries for more than twelve years. Email: mikewarren 4gzus@juno.com; website: www.4gzus.com

Toinette F. Welch has been married to the same wonderful man for 34 years and has two wonderful sons. Born and raised in Texas, she lived for many years in Germany, where she first encountered PWOC. God has always provided for her before she even knew she needed anything. Contact: welchjoh@hiwaay.net

Steven P. Wickstrom is an active duty Chief Warrant Officer in the U.S. Coast Guard. He was born in Indiana and has lived in Illinois, Michigan, California, North Carolina, Puerto Rico, and Hawaii. Due to the military lifestyle, he considers himself to be a professional nomad with saltwater in his veins and sand in his hair. He became a Christian at the age of eight and has written many articles for Christian websites. He is the author of *The Seagull Who Was Afraid to Fly*. His hobbies include writing, woodworking, and O gauge model railroading.

Jean Wise is a health commissioner and lives in Ohio. She has an active speaking and writing ministry. Her friend, Emily Curtis, has received hundreds of letters from troops serving in Iraq sharing stories of answered prayers. Contact: wiseguys@bright.net

Kimlee Saul Worrell loves the military lifestyle and opportunity to "go and teach all nations." She and husband, Hal, have four wonderful children. High school teacher, Family Readiness Group leader, PWOC local board member, and National Training Coordinator, Kim currently serves as PWOC-USA president. Email her at ksw4him247@ earthlink.net

Candy Zarcone, military wife since 1991 and active member of PWOC since 1995, enjoys the friends and traveling Army life makes possible. Her main pursuits are singing, teaching the Bible, and taking care of her three daughters. A published poet, this is her first published story. Email her at candyzhome@yahoo.com

About the Editors

Allison Bottke is the founder of God Allows U-Turns and lead editor in all the books developed under this popular umbrella brand. The international outreach includes books, tracts, logo merchandise, a line of greeting cards, a speaking ministry, and a charitable foundation. The God Allows U-Turns Foundation is donating a portion of all net profits from this volume to the Protestant Women of the Chapel. Visit the God Allows U-Turns website for more information on Allison and the exciting U-Turns outreach: www.godallowsuturns.com

Cheryll Hutchings is coeditor and administrative assistant of God Allows U-Turns. A Christian since the age of twelve, Cheryll has always let God lead her in life. The best adventure He's led her on so far has been joining God Allows U-Turns on the ground floor of the ministry when it began in 2000. Reading countless stories submitted by contributing authors from around the world, Cheryll has been instrumental in the development and editing of all books in the God Allows U-Turns series, as well as the most recent books in the new God Answers Prayers series. Scott, her 20-year-old son, is a corporal in the United States Marine Corps, serving in Iraq. She asks for your prayers in keeping him out of harm's way. Married to Bob for 27 years, Cheryll thanks him for his patience and understanding for the time she spends working on the U-Turns ministry. They also have a 23-year-old son named Aaron, who is working in the computer industry and plays his guitar in the church band. The Hutchings live in the country on several acres of seclusion, surrounded by the Lord's beautiful nature and wildlife.

Jennifer Devlin believes in the power of prayer. In 2002, God graciously chose to heal Jennifer of an incurable, long-term debilitating illness. He has called her to ministry to share His love with others. Currently residing at the Redstone Arsenal in Alabama where her husband recently served as the Garrison Commander, Jennifer and Army Colonel Robert Devlin have been married for 13 years and have a ten-year-old son, Owen. Jennifer's love of writing took her to a Christian writer's conference in New Mexico—where she met Allison Bottke, the founder of God Allows U-Turns. It was there Allison shared with Jennifer her longtime wish to develop a collection of military stories, and the rest as they say, is history. Jennifer has served on this military volume as coeditor, collaborator, and military liaison. She currently serves as the Southeast Regional Coordinator for PWOC, which encompasses over 45 installations of the Armed forces, including Cuba. She travels to train and build PWOC chapters for her region, as well as advising local chapters.

Ten Tips on How to Pray

1. Set aside a short time each day to meet with God. Yes, God hears our short "bullet prayers" throughout the day, but true fellowship wants more than that. Keep your appointment with God, just as you would any other appointment. Start by making these divine encounters brief. Even five minutes a day is a great start. You can add more time once the habit is established.

2. If you feel awkward at first, or your mind wanders, or you get a bit sleepy, don't feel guilty. God understands. Take a moment to read a few verses from the psalms or the day's entry in your favorite daily devotional book. It may take time to get used to being in the presence of God.

3. Ask God to help you pray. Prayer is, after all, His invention. He designed prayer as the means for us to communicate with Him. Let Him be your teacher.

4. One very good place to start praying is to simply confess any known sin to God and claim His forgiveness. At this same time, be sure you harbor no bitterness toward anyone else. Unforgiveness can hinder your prayers. If a specific person with whom you have hard feelings comes to mind, ask God to forgive

you and change your heart. If necessary, go to the other person and make things right.

5. Remember, prayer is more than asking for things. God loves it when we just take time to praise Him for who He is and thank Him for the blessings He's given us.

6. If you're likely to forget what you want to pray about, start a small written prayer list where you jot down the things you want to lift to the Lord.

7. Some people find it useful to write out their prayers and keep a journal of when and how God answers. For others, a journal may seem a distraction. Try it and see if it works for you.

8. Look for other opportunities to pray throughout the day. Waiting in line at the supermarket, washing the dishes, stuck in traffic...these are all excellent times to talk to God.

9. Remember the stories when people asked God to use them to touch another life. Ask God to do the same through you. Then watch for the divine appointments He will set up throughout the day.

10. Above all, consider your time with God a call to *joy*, not some staid, dry religious exercise. Learn to delight in God as you pray. He delights in you!

About *God Allows U-Turns*®

Along with the exciting Answered Prayer books published by Harvest House, we want to share with readers the entire scope of the powerful God Allows U-Turns outreach of hope and healing.

The broad outreach of this organization includes the book you now hold in your hands, as well as other nonfiction and fiction books for adults, youth, and children. Written by Allison Gappa Bottke, along with other collaborating authors and coeditors, there are currently 17 books available under the God Allows U-Turns umbrella brand, with additional books releasing soon, including Allison's first novel in the "chick-lit" genre.

More than 50,000 copies of the God Allows U-Turns tract, featuring Allison's powerful testimony of making a u-turn toward God, have been distributed around the world.

There is a line of nine God Allows U-Turns greeting cards touching on difficult times when new direction is needed. Also available is an entire line of merchandise featuring the highly recognizable God Allows U-Turns signature yellow road sign, items such as Bible book covers, ball caps, and such. Also in development is a God Allows U-Turns TV interview talk show and a national speakers tour.

Sharing the life-saving message that you can never be so lost or so broken that you can't turn toward God is Allison's main passion in her life and in her ministry.

Visit your local bookstore or the God Allows U-Turns website to find out more about this exciting ministry that is helping to change lives: www.godallowsuturns.com or write:

Allison Bottke
God Allows U-Turns®
P.O. Box 717
Faribault, MN 55021-0717

Contact: editor@godallowsuturns.com

The God Allows U-Turns® Foundation

ONE OF THE MOST PROFOUND lessons in the Bible is that of giving. The Holy Bible is quite clear in teaching us how we are to live our lives. Scripture refers to this often, and never has the need to share with others been so great.

Give, and it will be given to you. A good measure, pressed down, shaken together and running over, will be poured into your lap. For with the measure you use, it will be measured to you (Luke 6:38).

In keeping with the lessons taught us by the Lord our God, we are pleased to donate a portion of the net profits of every God Allows U-Turns book to one or more nonprofit Christian charities. These donations are made through the God Allows U-Turns Foundation, a funding mechanism established by Kevin and Allison Bottke as a way to share the success of the growing U-Turns outreach ministry.

For more details visit the website at:
www.godallowsuturns.com

God Answers Prayers

THE STORIES YOU HAVE READ in this volume we
mitted by readers just like you. From the very start
inspiring and compelling book series, it has been o
to encourage people from around the world to subn
publication their slice-of-life, true short stories of
God answers prayers. Please visit the God Allows
Turns website at www.godallowsuturns.com for infor
tion on upcoming volumes in development, as well as
writer's guidelines and deadlines.

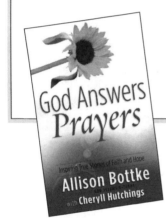

GOD ANSWERS PRAYERS

These testimonies focus on timeless,
universal themes such as love, forgiveness, salvation, and hope, and provide a
powerful and passionate look at how
prayer can inspire, encourage, change,
and heal.

ISBN-13: 978-0-7369-1587-8
ISBN-10: 0-7369-1587-7
Paperback

GOD ANSWERS MOMS' PRAYERS

Moms who send their children into the
world surrounded by prayer every day
will appreciate this tribute to the most
faithful of prayer warriors. This collection of true stories inspires women to
combine their love with faith, hope,
prayer, and confidence. Whether moms
offer prayers of thanksgiving or desperate cries for help, God answers
in profound and poignant ways.

ISBN-13: 978-0-7369-1588-5
ISBN-10: 0-7369-1588-5
Paperback

re sub-
of this
r goal
it for
how
U-
na-
for

.ife but the demands of family, work, and
itions. Elizabeth George, bestselling author
o deeper communication with God.

) PRAYER

.oung Woman After God's Own Heart, offers another
r own journey, the Bible, and the lives of others,
ve power and dynamic impact of prayer on everyday

.iANGES EVERYTHING™

itinues to provide her audience with books that touch the
warmly invites readers into her own life as she chooses to
of her circumstances. The Prayer That Changes Everything™ is
ersonal stories, biblical truths, and practical guiding principles
onders that take place when Christians offer praise in the middle
orrow, fear, and, yes, abundance and joy.

R OF A PRAYING® WIFE
artian

iares how wives can develop a deeper relationship with their husbands
ig for them. Packed with practical advice on praying for specific areas,
ig: decision–making, fears, spiritual strength, and sexuality, women will
er the fulfilling marriage God intended.

. POWER OF A PRAYING® HUSBAND
rmie Omartian

uilding on the success of The Power of a Praying® Wife (more than 1 million copies
sold), Stormie offers this guide to help husbands pray more effectively for their
wives. Packed with real–life examples and refreshing honesty regarding her own
marriage, The Power of a Praying® Husband encourages men to lovingly intercede
for their wives in every area.

THE REMARKABLE PRAYERS OF THE BIBLE
Jim George

Jim George looks deeply into the prayers of some great people in the Bible—and
shares what readers can learn from others who loved God and desired to follow
Him wholeheartedly. They will discover the many practical lessons contained in
these thought–provoking prayers.